GEOLOGY
PROJECTS FOR YOUNG SCIENTISTS

BRUCE SMITH AND
DAVID MCKAY

GEOLOGY PROJECTS FOR YOUNG SCIENTISTS

PROJECTS FOR YOUNG SCIENTISTS
FRANKLIN WATTS
NEW YORK / CHICAGO / LONDON / TORONTO / SYDNEY

THE AUTHORS DEDICATE THIS BOOK TO THEIR MOTHERS,
MARIE SMITH AND PHYLLIS MCKAY,
WITH LOVE.

Photographs copyright © : NASA: pp. 11, 73 top; Monkmeyer Press
Photos: pp. 19 (Mimi Forsyth), 85 (Hufnagle); Jerold Stoflet: p. 36;
American Museum of Natural History, Photographic Collection: pp. 39
(C. Schuberth, #332968), 43 top right (Charles H. Coles, #316057), 43
center left (Rota, #2A9041), 43 center right (Lee Boltin, #322265), 43
bottom (#13397), 122 (Schuberth, #335727), 123 (Schuberth, #335730);
U.S. Geological Survey, Photographic Library: pp. 43 top left (F. C.
Calkins), 88, 89 (G. Plafker), 91 (R. E. Wallace), 96, 100 top (C. Milton), 100
center (H. T. Stearns), 100 bottom; Fundamental Photographs/Richard
Megna: p. 57; Photo Researchers Inc./Manuel Grossberg: p. 62; Cold
Spring Harbor Laboratories/Susan Lauter: p. 67; Upjohn Company/H. M.
Einspahn: p. 73 bottom; Sierra Club, Colby Library, San Francisco, CA:
pp. 79 top (Joseph N. LeConte), 79 bottom; Bruce Smith: p. 101; U.S.
Army Corps of Engineers/James N. Sanders: p. 115.

Library of Congress Cataloging-in-Publication Data

Smith, Bruce G.
Geology projects for young scientists / Bruce Smith and David
McKay.
p.   cm. — (Projects for young scientists)
Includes bibliographical references and index.
Summary: Projects and experiments explore such aspects of the
Earth as its age, plate tectonics, earthquakes, and hydrogeology.
ISBN 0-531-11012-5 (lib. bdg.)   ISBN 0-531-15651-6 (pbk.)
1. Geology—Experiments—Juvenile literature. [1. Geology—
Experiments. 2. Experiments.] I. McKay, David W. II. Title.
III. Series.
QE44.S65   1992
550'.78—dc20   91-43705 CIP AC

CONTENTS

ACKNOWLEDGMENTS

The authors wish to express their gratitude to their wives, Pam Smith and Mary McKay, without whose support and tolerance this book would not have been completed.

Many thanks also to Henry Rasof, our editor, whose diligence and patience not only assured the success of this project but also allowed the authors to acquire a taste for octopus.

Finally, appreciation is due our loyal colleagues and energetic students for their inspiration and help along the way.

1

WHAT ON EARTH
IS GEOLOGY?

Imagine an intelligent life-form positioned on a body in space. The size and mass of the body are huge compared with the size and mass of the life-form. The body is almost 8,000 miles (13,000 kilometers, or km) in diameter, over 600 billion billion tons in mass. (That's a six with twenty zeros after it!) From a long distance away this body looks smooth, but up close it turns out to have peaks over 5 miles (8 km) high and trenches over 6 miles (10 km) deep.

This body is composed of different types of substances, including hard ones and soft ones, heavy and light ones, liquids and gases. In fact, thousands upon thousands of different types of substances can be found at or near the surface. Under the surface of the body are layers of various compositions and thicknesses, including layers of hot, molten material under crushing pressures and at temperatures over 10,000°F (5,600°C). At the very center of the body is an extremely dense, hot metal core surrounded by a layer of molten rocklike material. About this inner region is a thick layer of heavy rock covered by a thin surface layer of rocks.

The surface is constantly changing. Some of the changes are slow but can cause dramatic movements of large sections of the surface. Pieces of the surface collide as they move, causing vibrations to shudder throughout the entire body. Sometimes the heat and pressure inside the body cause hot, molten material to shoot out onto the surface. At times, surface material is forced back into the interior of the body to be remelted and reformed.

Forces surround this body and affect everything around it, including the life-form. One force pulls everything toward the center of the body. Another force attracts objects made of iron. Some of the materials in the body undergo radioactive decay and give off various types of particles and rays. This radioactivity also produces much of the heat at the interior of the body. Imagine, too, that this body is spinning around a central axis and flying through space at thousands of miles an hour around a huge ball of hot gases.

Now, what if you were that life-form? What if you had an opportunity to explore and study such a place? What exciting and wonderful things could you find? Where would you start, and how would you proceed?

Of course, you are that being. The strange, wonderful body is the Earth, which you can see viewed from space in Figure 1. And investigations of the body called Earth are part of the science of geology. Geologists study the physical history of the Earth, the materials it comprises, and the physical changes it has undergone and is undergoing. Although professional geologists have formal training and degrees in their discipline, in a way we are all geologists. We spend our lives learning how the complex and fascinating planet known as Earth works and how it affects our lives. We cannot separate our lives from the study of the planet we live on.

This book will provide you with opportunities, in the form of science projects, to more clearly understand the Earth, to become a better earth scientist. Some of these

Figure 1 The Earth as seen from *Apollo 17*

projects will allow you to explore the actual substances in the Earth and how they behave. Others will involve making models to better understand these substances and the forces that affect them—and you.

The projects are often suitable for classroom assignments or for science fairs. Many are suitable for home investigations as well, but be sure to get the permission of both a science teacher and an adult in your family.

Some projects include detailed instructions, while others include hints or suggestions only. For both types of projects, however, you are encouraged to find your own way of doing things, provided it is safe and has the approval of a knowledgeable science teacher.

THE SCIENCE OF GEOLOGY

As a science, geology bears many resemblances to other sciences such as chemistry, biology, and physics. Like chemists, biologists, and physicists, geologists make observations, try to explain their observations, and test their explanations. But unique to geology is the fact that although many experiments are performed in the confines of a laboratory, the setting for much of the practice of this science is the entire Earth: In a sense, the geologist's laboratory includes the Earth itself.

SCIENCE PROJECTS

You probably have some notion of what a science project is: an open-ended investigation of something to do with science. Such an investigation typically can involve performing an experiment in which you test some ideas you have; building a model; doing library research; doing surveys and interviews; or making a collection. A project can be just one of these, or two or more.

This book includes a variety of projects. Some have

detailed instructions and a fair amount of background information. Others have sketchy directions and no background. Still other projects are really best described by the word "idea." These are ideas or questions for you to think about and to try to answer in your own way. What most of the projects have in common is that for the most part they are open-ended investigations. No answers are given, even to obvious questions.

GEOLOGY PROJECTS

Two aspects of geology which make science projects unique is size and time. Many geologic phenomena are so large that studying them in their totality is almost impossible. However, scale models can be used with great success. Also, many geologic processes require tremendous amounts of time to observe: millions or even billions of years. These amounts of "deep time" are obviously well beyond our experience. Therefore, we must attempt to grasp these concepts through analogies or by looking at smaller segments of time. In this, geology is similar to astronomy.

THE SCIENTIFIC
PROCESS

Whether a scientist is investigating a very particular problem or a more general problem, he or she should be open to new ideas and directions. If something looks interesting, the scientist will investigate it or consider it for a future investigation. Curiosity is a hallmark of the good scientist, and following one's nose is often how great discoveries are made.

For example, one of the leading theories of why dinosaurs became extinct was developed because a scientist, Luis Alvarez, became curious about a particular layer of sediments he found. From this discovery and his skills as a scientist, the theory of a great meteorite impact causing the extinctions was born.

Serendipity, the art of taking advantage of discoveries that happen by chance, is also a factor in a good many scientific achievements. Although you will read and hear a lot about "the scientific method," especially in science textbooks, the fact is that there are many scientific methods. All scientific inquiry has a few things in common, but scientists work in different ways, and often chance plays as great a role in an investigation as rigorous methods. Good science is basically about looking for the truth, and it is about disproving falsehoods. It doesn't matter whether you work in the lab, in the library, in space, or on a mountaintop, as long as your goal is to discover the truth. If you discover something that you can't prove, or that someone else disproves, then you must recognize that your discovery is probably not the truth after all. But even if an experiment flops or your hypotheses or ideas prove wrong, you shouldn't feel like a failure: proving something wrong is as much a success as proving something right.

If in doing or considering one of the projects in this book you notice or think of something more interesting than the project at hand, you may want to consider switching the direction of your investigations—being sure to consult with a knowledgeable adult. Quite possibly your hunch may lead you in a direction never before explored. At worst, you will have the satisfaction of developing your own project and seeing where it leads. And most likely, doing your own thing will be more exciting than simply following someone else's directions. For if anything, the projects in this book should be viewed not as fixed investigations whose directions must be strictly adhered to, but rather as motivational tools to get you thinking. So, always be on the lookout for the unexpected.

Although planning is necessary to do a scientifically oriented project, you can learn a lot, in a more informal way, by just keeping your eyes open. For example, if you are on a trip, watch the surrounding countryside carefully. Road cuts often expose interesting rock formations. Road-side parks give a good opportunity to get close to the rocks. If you are on a rafting trip, observe how the river has cut through the surrounding rocks. If you are flying, you can get a good view of the nature of a whole area. You can see mountain ranges, rivers, and lakes. In short, always be aware of the Earth around you and try to learn as much about it as you can.

WORKING SCIENTIFICALLY

Since a key part of a geologist's work is observation, a key part of the research for your geology project will be good observations. Whether you are working in the library, in your classroom laboratory, or in the field, you will want to take careful notice of what you see and record your observations in a notebook, as shown in Figure 2. You also should keep track of your methods and ideas, as well as of information found in articles and other books. Date all entries and include any sketches or drawings you make.

Keeping a notebook is not only standard laboratory practice. Often it is required for projects for many classroom assignments and science fairs.

In addition to taking notes and making drawings, you may wish to document your methods and observations with photographs. Any camera can be used, but a 35mm camera with slide film gives the best results. Slides are very effective, and they can be made into prints if necessary. If you are creative, photographs might even be the basis of a project. Imagine, for example, being able to document the eruption of a volcano or the destructive effects of an earthquake!

If you have access to a video camera, you might want to make videos instead of, or in addition to, photographs.

FIELD NOTES

SATURDAY, MAY 6, 1990

SAMPLE #17 – APPROX. 2" x 3" BROKEN OFF A LARGER ROCK
OUTCROP ABOUT 6' x 15'. SAMPLE IS LIGHT–COLORED, PINK
AND WHITE MINERALS WITH SOME DARKER MICA MINERALS
(POSSIBLY MUSCOUITE). SAMPLE IS PROBABLY GRANITE.
SITE OF COLLECTION IS APPROXIMATELY 200 YARDS SOUTH
OF HWY. 10 BEHIND GREENVILLE SCHOOL IN THE TOWN OF
HORTONVILLE. LAND OWNED BY JOHN JONES. I RECEIVED
PERMISSION TO COLLECT ROCKS ON HIS LAND.

ROAD CUT – LOCATED ON HWY. 10, 5 MILES NORTHEAST OF
HORTONVILLE. APPEARS TO BE LIMESTONE. LAYERS ARE
HORIZONTAL ALMOST WITH A 50° DIP.

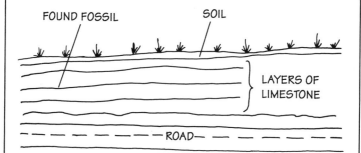

SAMPLE #18
SMALL FOSSIL OF BEACHWOOD FOUND AT ROADCUT
DESCRIBED ABOVE. ABOUT 1" x 1/4".

TESTED THE ROCK WITH DILUTE HYDROCHLORIC
ACID AND IT BUBBLED.

Figure 2 Sample page from a field notebook

SOURCES OF INFORMATION

An important aspect of the study of earth science is research. Become familiar with books, articles, and publications related to earth science. Libraries are a good place to start. However, to get specific, detailed information about a particular location, you may have to contact more specialized sources. A very good source is the United States Geological Survey (USGS). The USGS can provide thousands of publications on all aspects of earth science. Most states have a state geological survey that publishes information about the geology of the state. Local geology clubs or historical societies and the earth science or geology department at a local college or university are another great source. Rock and mineral clubs can put you in contact with many people with detailed knowledge about the rocks in a local area. The Appendix of this book lists a number of useful sources and publications.

SAFETY

Safety is the most important ingredient in a scientific investigation. Good organization and planning, neatness, and safe science practices will allow you to devote all your creative energies to the investigations themselves.

• **Make safety your top priority.** The information here and elsewhere in this book will help you accomplish this aim. Instructions and safety cautions are based on recent, reliable information but cannot possibly cover all possible situations. You must exercise your own good judgment and rely on your teacher or other adults.

• **Do *all* projects under the supervision of a qualified science teacher or other knowledgeable adult.** This is especially important since many of the projects in this book have minimal directions.

• **Follow instructions and heed safety cautions given in this book and by your supervisor.** If in doubt, check with a teacher. Work carefully. A careless or apathetic attitude toward safety may lead to a serious accident. Knowledge and preparation are the keys to controlling hazards.

• **Be especially careful working in the field.** While collecting samples, be careful when climbing on rock piles so you don't injure yourself or others below you if you should dislodge loose rocks. Be careful near cliffs or quarry walls. Overhanging rocks may fall without warning. Abandoned mines and quarries are extremely dangerous. Always keep away from active quarry operations, since blasting and machinery are very dangerous. Do not venture into unfamiliar areas alone.

• **Protect your eyes, ears, face, hands, and body while conducting experiments, as shown in Figure 3.** *Wear approved safety goggles or a face shield at all times.* Wear earplugs if your project may be noisy. Wear protective gloves and a plastic apron to protect your hands and body against spills.

• **Powdered minerals may be toxic, so use a dust mask when working with finely divided materials.**

• **Be especially careful working with chemicals.** Many chemicals are poisonous or flammable or give off irritating fumes. Don't wear contact lenses. Work in a well-ventilated area and wash your hands and all equipment after you are through working with chemicals. Never touch or taste chemicals.

• **Keep your work space neat and organized.** Sloppiness can lead to accidents.

• **Know where you can get help fast in case of an emergency.**

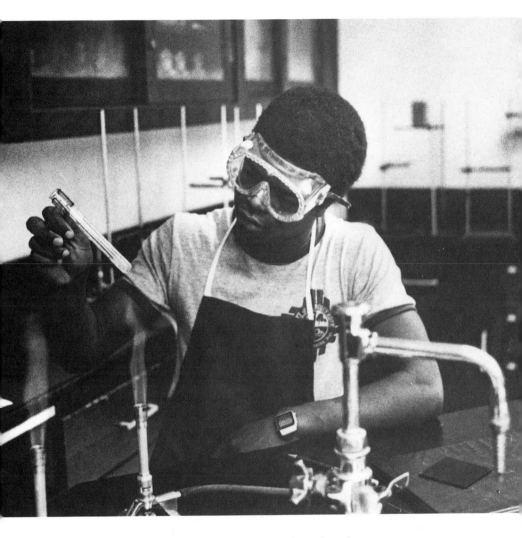

Figure 3 When doing experiments, always wear approved safety goggles and a lab apron and keep your work space clean. When heating chemicals in a test tube, always point the test tube away from you and from other people.

MY NEIGHBORHOOD GEOLOGICAL SURVEY (MNGS)

A good project to get you started studying the Earth is to make your own geological survey. A geological survey is a description of the rocks, soils, topography, water, and other related characteristics of a specific area. Geological surveys are an important part of what earth scientists do. One of the first activities many states and countries do is commission geological surveys of the land. The famous Lewis and Clark expedition to the Northwest Territories was primarily a geological survey to determine the extent and nature of the newly acquired land. Your geological survey will be a simple description of the immediate area where you live.

In your geological survey, first describe the area you will report on. Describe the boundaries and map the area. Include in the report everything you can determine about the land surface—how much is rock, grass, concrete, buildings, soil, etc. Identify rock outcrops, if any. Take notes and make drawings or take pictures of any interesting features. Try to obtain aerial photos or satellite images of the area. Maybe even develop a field-trip guide for the area or a slide presentation about the geology of your neighborhood. People often think that they need to travel long distances to observe geological phenomena, but often some interesting things can be right in our own areas.

Learning about the piece of Earth we are closest to is an important first step toward the understanding of the Earth as a whole. Have fun!

2

MEASURING THE EARTH

From ancient times to the present, human beings have investigated the planet Earth, seeking to describe its physical characteristics and to explain the processes that formed it and continue to change it.

Over the years, questions have included: What shape is the Earth? How big is it? How great is its mass? Are these characteristics changing? Although accurate answers are now known, arriving at these answers is instructive and challenging. In addition, since one of the tenets of science is to accept only what can be proved, making some measurements of your own is a good way not only to learn how such measurements are made but to find out whether the values given in books are correct. In this chapter you will learn how to make some basic measurements and observations which can be used to answer the most basic questions: What is the shape of the Earth? How big is the Earth? How much does the Earth weigh?

THE SHAPE OF THE EARTH

In the ancient world, there were few experimental scientists, but many of the same philosophers who speculated about the nature of the mind and the nature of existence also speculated about the nature of the physical world. These philosophers had different ideas about the shape of the Earth. At one time or another, they thought the Earth was shaped like a cube, a sphere, a cylinder, a flat disk, or even the back of a turtle. To this day there is a group of people who belong to a group called The Flat Earth Society. What is the shape of the Earth and how do we know?

Finding the Shape of the Earth

To determine the shape of the Earth, you will need to make observations near a large body of water such as an ocean, or a lake at least 5 miles (8 km) across. You also will need a map of the area where you are going to make the observations, a magnetic compass, and a pair of binoculars.

Go to the shore of the large body of water. Because you are going to observe objects in the distance over the water, try to do this on a clear, calm day. Locate your position on the map. Using first your naked eye and then the binoculars, view the horizon over the body of water, as shown in Figure 4, noting any objects on the water surface, for example, ships, small boats, islands, buoys, or the opposite shore line. Using the map and compass, determine the direction of the object and draw a line on the map from your position to the object. Carefully record your observations about the objects, especially the height.

From those observations, what can you conclude about the shape of the Earth?

For Further Investigation

•   Can you use your observations of a moving ship on the water to determine whether the Earth is curved?

•   If you cannot get to a large body of water, can you do the above experiments anyway?

•   During a boat trip, could you make any observations that would reveal the shape of the Earth?

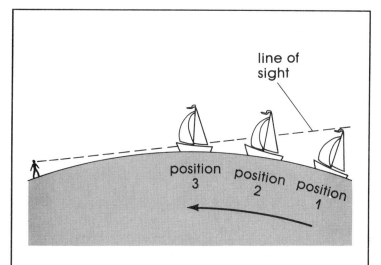

Figure 4 How a ship would be viewed as it approached an observer on a curved surface. Would you make this same observation if you were looking at a ship on an ocean or lake?

• Do some research on using triangulation to describe the shape of the Earth and prepare a historical project. Compare your experimental findings with those of earlier scientists.

• Research other beliefs about the shape of the Earth. Find out about The Flat Earth Society. Why do people belong to this group? A survey of people in your community might yield some interesting results.

• Read Edwin A. Abbott's *Flatland* (New York: Penguin, 1987), a book about a flat world inhabited by flat creatures. Also read A. K. Dewdney's *The Planiverse: Computer Contact with a Two-Dimensional World* (New York: Poseidon Press, 1984), a more recent book about creatures discovered on a computer screen, an "update" of Abbott. Do these authors accurately describe the worlds they have "discovered"? What do you think the world would be like if it were indeed flat?

Using a Lunar Eclipse to Find the Shape of the Earth

Like any object that interrupts light, the Earth casts a shadow. This shadow can be observed at night during a lunar eclipse, when the Earth passes between the sun and the moon. From the shape of the shadow you should be able to corroborate what you already may know about the shape of the Earth.

Eclipses of the moon are not as infrequent as you might think. Look up the dates and times of the next few lunar eclipses in your locale. If you cannot observe an actual eclipse, an alternative is to study detailed photographs of past eclipses.

Eclipses are best observed in a flat area away from lights. However, a clear night is the most important ingredient. A pair of binoculars will come in handy, as will a 35mm camera with a telephoto lens, high-speed film, and a tripod.

When the eclipse is visible, observe it with the naked eye or with binoculars. Sketch the shadow and note the sharpness of the shadow as it progresses across the disk of the moon. If you are using a camera, take a sequence of photos throughout the entire eclipse. For information on suitable shutter speeds and f-stops, consult a photography book or experienced photographer.

What can you conclude about the shape of the Earth from your observations? Do you have enough evidence to unequivocally state what shape the Earth is?

In 450 B.C., a philosopher named Anaxagoras observed a lunar eclipse and concluded that the Earth was spherical. But couldn't a disk or a cylinder also cast a shadow such as the one you observed? Why was Anaxagoras so sure of himself?

Making a Model of the Earth

Make a model of the Earth showing its "exact" shape. If your Earth is a sphere, is it a perfect sphere? If the answer is yes, why is it perfect? If the answer is no, why is it irregular?

• Find out what happens to a sphere, cube, or prism made of very pliable clay when you spin it. You could use an electric drill or small battery-powered motor to spin some clay shapes. Do some research on any connections that might exist between the shape and rotation of the Earth.

Historic Voyages

Over the centuries, explorers have set out in search of new lands, often guided by misinformation. Assemble a historical display chronicling the voyages by air, sea, or space that have helped determine the shape of the Earth. Be sure to include a chronology of developments in the relevant technology. Why did it take so long to prove the actual shape of the Earth?

THE SHAPES OF OTHER
HEAVENLY BODIES

Some geologists specialize in studies of the moon and other celestial bodies. Planetary geologists study processes which take place on other planets. They study the size, mass, and shape of the planets. Sometimes, as in the case of the planet Pluto, size, distance, accurate measurements were a long time in coming.

• Investigate, through experimentation and library research, the shapes of these other objects that are part of our solar system. Compare your findings with those for Earth. See if you can deduce some general rules governing the shapes of these heavenly bodies.

• Astronomers study these heavenly bodies in addition to the sun. They also study objects and phenomena beyond the solar system, including other stars, star clusters, nebulae, and galaxies. Do some research on the shapes of these objects. Is there a connection between shape and speed of rotation?

THE SIZE OF THE EARTH

What are the circumference and diameter of the Earth? How does one go about measuring something larger than any known instrument? Can you figure out a way to measure the size of the Earth? Are your answers close to the accepted measurements? If they are different, how would you explain the discrepancies? Can you improve on your method?

Using Eratosthenes's Method to Find the Size of the Earth

Eratosthenes was a Greek scholar who lived from about 275 to 195 B.C. One of his most important contributions was to calculate the circumference of the Earth. His method was based on the observation that the position of the sun varies when the sun is observed from different locations at the same time of the year. This variation, Eratosthenes hypothesized, was a result of the curvature of the Earth's surface. Observation of the sun's position can be used to determine the size of the Earth.

MATERIALS

A hammer, a straight stick about 3 feet (1 meter, or m) long, 6 feet (2 m) of string, a thumbtack, a protractor, a watch, and a map of the Earth.

PROCEDURE

To measure the angle of the sun's rays, choose a bright, sunny day to work on and a flat, open area away from shadows of buildings or trees. Find an area of soft ground and use the hammer to pound the stick a short way into the ground so that it stands straight up. Attach the string to the top of the stick with the thumbtack. Use the protractor to make sure the angle between the stick and the ground is 90 degrees.

Observe the shadow of stick on the ground and mark the end of the shadow. Stretch the string from the top of the stick to the end of the shadow. Measure the angle, a, between the string and the stick. Figure 5 shows a schematic of the setup.

In order to measure the circumference of the Earth, you need two such sun angle measurements taken at the same time great distances apart. Since this is impractical, you can measure the angle of the sun at a time of the year when you know the exact latitudes on Earth where the sun is directly overhead at noon. At this location, the stick would cast no shadow and the angle of the shadow would therefore be zero. It is then easy to use your shadow angle to determine the size of the Earth. (Hint: There are four dates on which we know the exact latitudes at which the sun is directly overhead at noon local time.)

Using a world map, you can determine the distance between your location and that of the point where the sun is directly overhead. Figure 6 will help you calculate the circumference of the Earth. In this drawing, the angle a is the angle between the string and the stick in the first part of the experiment. It is the same as the angle formed by a line from the center of the Earth to the position of the stick and a line from the center of the Earth to the point where the vertical rays of the sun are striking the Earth. The distance d represents the distance over the surface of the Earth between those two points.

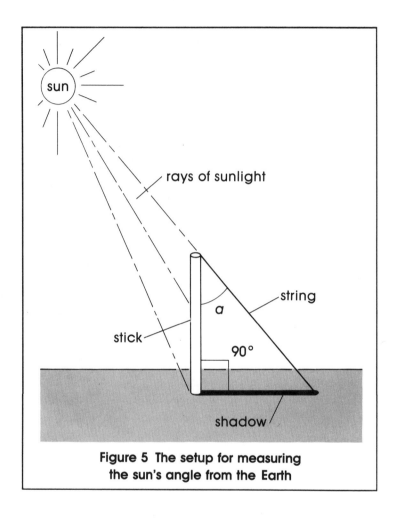

Figure 5 The setup for measuring the sun's angle from the Earth

The circumference of the Earth can be calculated by using the formula

$$\text{circumference of the Earth} = \frac{360 \times d}{a},$$

where 360 is the total number of degrees in a circle.

Compare your figures with those of Eratosthenes and of modern scientists.

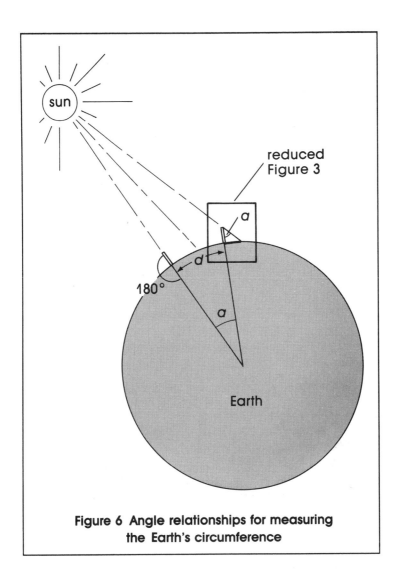

**Figure 6 Angle relationships for measuring
the Earth's circumference**

For Further Investigation

• If you aren't happy with your figures, see if you can get better results by modifying the setup.

• Does this method have any other applications?

—29—

Using the Stars to Measure the Earth's Circumference

Develop a method of measuring the circumference of the Earth using observations of stars. Compare your results with those obtained by other methods. Does this method have any other applications?

Other Investigations of Measurements

If you know the circumference of the Earth, can you find its diameter and radius? Are these two figures always the same regardless of where you are on Earth? Look into the concept of average diameter and radius.

If you are an astronomy buff, find out how measurements are made of other objects in space, from dust particles to galaxies. Can you make some of these measurements yourself? If you lived on another planet, how would you go about measuring the Earth?

THE MASS OF THE EARTH

The mass of an object is a measure of the amount of matter contained in the object. According to Newton's law of gravitation, the strength of the gravitational field of an object is proportional to the mass of the object. When we weigh ourselves, we are really measuring the force of attraction between ourselves and the Earth. In other words, our weight is a function not only of our mass but of the Earth's mass as well. We are really weighing the Earth as well as ourselves. The mass of the Earth, through its gravitational force, affects all other masses around it.

Using a Pendulum to Find the Mass of the Earth

Knowing what you now know about the concepts of mass and weight, could you measure the mass of the Earth without having to actually place the Earth on a scale? One way to do this is with a pendulum, an object suspended by a long cord or wire long enough to allow it to swing freely. The pendulum swings back and forth, and how it swings depends on how gravity pulls on it.

MATERIALS

About 8 to 10 ounces (250–400 grams, or g) of clay, 3 feet (1 m) of string, a yardstick or meterstick, a stopwatch, a calculator (optional), and a spreadsheet computer program (optional).

PROCEDURE

Make the pendulum weight from the clay and attach it to a support with the string. After you measure and record the distance from the pivot to the bottom of the ball, pull the ball back about a foot (30 cm) and let it swing. Determine how long the pendulum takes to make twenty full swings and divide this value by 20 to give the period of the pendulum. Repeat the procedure using various arcs of swing and find the average period of the pendulum. Using this data and appropriate equations you find in a physics book, calculate the acceleration, g, due to gravity.

Calculate the radius of the Earth using the figure you found earlier for the circumference. Then use the figures you have to determine the mass of the Earth. Compare your results with the figures given in books. How close did you get?

For Further Investigation

Modify the apparatus to improve the accuracy of your results.

• Find out if the mass of the Earth is evenly distributed.

• You can use the same apparatus to measure the strength of the gravitational force anywhere on the Earth. Try doing this project on the top floor of a high building. If you have the opportunity, time the pendulum at different locations and compare your results.

- Would such a device work on other planets?

- Do research on methods to find the mass of other astronomical objects, such as distant galaxies. Conversely, if you were an extraterrestrial, how would you go about measuring the mass of the Earth from your distant planet? From a spaceship orbiting Earth?

- Investigate the gravitational attraction between bodies in space.

DOES THE EARTH ROTATE ON AN AXIS?

You probably have heard that the Earth rotates on an axis and that this is the reason we have day and night. But can you prove this? The answer may lie in the experiments that follow in the next paragraph.

If you have ever visited a science museum, you may have seen a Foucault pendulum. A long wire reaches down from the ceiling and is attached to a large metal ball. Below it is a circle divided into segments. The pendulum always swings in the same plane, but if you watch its movements long enough you will notice that the circle is turning.

Construct your own Foucault pendulum and try to answer the following questions: What does such a pendulum demonstrate? Can what it demonstrates be proven in other ways? Will such a pendulum swing the same way no matter where it is on Earth, even if you are on top of the highest mountain or deep undersea or underground?

For Further Investigation
- If you are interested in literature as well as science, you might want to read a recent novel by an Italian novelist, Umberto Eco, called *Foucault's Pendulum*.

- If the Earth does indeed spin on an axis, could you

use the rotation to run any machines? Couldn't you design a perpetual-motion machine in this way?

• If the Earth does rotate, is the rotation at a constant speed? Has it always rotated at this speed? If the rotation is slowing down or speeding up, what is the cause?

• Read up on the Coriolis force and investigate the relationship between this force and things that rotate or move in other ways on Earth, for example, winds, waves, and airplanes, etc. Can the Coriolis force be used to do work, as "work" is defined by physicists?

• Investigate the rotation of other heavenly bodies and of other objects, for example, subatomic particles. Do electrons really spin on an axis? What does electron spin measure? What happens when an electron spins? When a planet spins? When a magnet spins?

3

COLLECTING AND STUDYING PIECES OF THE EARTH

Now that you have some appreciation of the larger features of the Earth, you may want to become better acquainted with the smaller features, the nitty-gritty, so to speak. What is the nitty-gritty of the Earth? The water, the air, and, or course, the rocks and minerals.

Studying pieces of the Earth is not only instructive; it is fun and fascinating. In addition, it will make you better appreciate the importance throughout history of better understanding the nature and value of rocks and minerals. Fortunes have been made and lost on minerals, or on what people thought were minerals. For instance, when conquering South America, the Spaniards came across large nuggets of a white metal that was heavy like gold but the wrong color. They threw the large nuggets away, failing to understand that the metal was platinum, now much more valuable than gold!

MAKING A COLLECTION

Collecting samples is an important part of the work of many geologists. If you are interested in geology, or think you might be, most likely you will want to start your own collection of rocks and minerals. Like a stamp collection, a rock and mineral collection is fun to maintain. It is nice to look at and show to other people, it can be a science project in itself and it can provide the raw materials for numerous other science projects. Even if you don't plan to become a geologist, collecting rocks, minerals, gems, and fossils from different places can grow into a relaxing, rewarding, long-term hobby. It is a great way to learn more about the Earth. Figure 7 shows part of an "amateur" rock collection.

However, there are collections, and there are collections. That is, some collections are simply a random assortment of specimens, while other collections have a purpose. A random collection has its pleasures, but it will not impress a teacher or science fair judge looking for purpose.

If you want to satisfy a requirement, you will need to collect with a purpose in mind. Collecting specimens in order to construct an exhibit showing the nature of the geologic materials in your area would be a good project for certain assignments, but it isn't doing an experiment, if an experiment is what you need to do. However, an extensive exhibit, complete with original sketches, maps, photographs, etc., could still be impressive, even if, most likely, it wouldn't garner you a prize in the Westinghouse Science Talent Search.

On the other hand, you might be able to come up with a hypothesis that could be tested by looking for certain specimens you predict you will find: "If such and such is true, then I should find gold in the ground behind the deli on Main Street." This is more the way someone like a petroleum geologist might work, using scientific principles for practical purposes.

But if you need a "real" experiment, a collection could serve your purposes, as you will see later in this chapter with the testing of samples for physical properties. In these

Figure 7 Quality, not quantity, is what counts
in many endeavors, including a rock collection.

projects, experiments are done with the specimens you have collected.

So a collection of rocks or other Earth materials can be simply a collection, or it can serve as a springboard to more-involved projects that include lab experimentation as well. Many specific project ideas with Earth materials can be found in these two books: Vinson Browns's *Building Your Own Nature Museum for Study and Pleasure* (New York: Arco, 1984), and Ruth MacFarlane's *Making Your Own Nature Museum* (New York: Franklin Watts, 1989).

THE ART OF COLLECTING

Before you begin collecting, for whatever purpose, you will need to know a few things so that you don't just end up with a box full of rocks. Such a "collection" would be less than useless.

Where to Obtain Specimens
Does a relative or friend have a collection? If so, you might start by asking him or her if you could inherit or borrow it. Talk to other collectors to find out the best spots near you for finding rocks and minerals. Books and maps, sometimes published by states and available at no charge, and field guides are also valuable resources; some of these are listed in the For Further Reading section at the back of this book.

Almost any location, even the middle of a big city, is worth searching for rocks and minerals, *as long as collecting is permitted, you have permission to collect, and the circumstances are safe.* These locations include public lands such as parks, campgrounds, recreation areas, waysides, and monuments, as long as collecting is permitted. Many good places to collect specimens are on private land, including rock quarries, gravel pits, open fields, wooded areas, even your own backyard. Other places to try include building excavations; road cuts, which may expose rock masses or boulders; monument works; gravel pits; smelters' premises; vacant lots; beaches (especially pebble beaches); the shores of lakes and rivers; and stream beds. Figure 8 shows one such location.

You can also obtain specimens from stores (rock and gift shops, science museum stores, etc.) and from individuals. In fact, at places like national parks and monuments, state parks, and some beaches, collecting may be forbidden. If so, you will have to purchase specimens at stores. At Petrified Forest National Park in Arizona, for example, where collectors are asked upon leaving the park to return any specimens they have collected, you can purchase petrified wood and other specimens at the visitor centers or outside the park at private concessions.

Many people launch their collections with the purchase or gift of an inexpensive collection, and they may expand their collection by trading with other collectors. It is particularly fun to trade with people who live in another part of the United States or in a different country. Rocks and minerals that are common in your area might be quite rare somewhere else and vice versa.

And finally, the April issue of a monthly magazine called *Lapidary Journal* (1094 Cudahy Place, San Diego, CA 92110) lists the names of dealers and other sources of rocks and minerals.

Do's and Don'ts of Collecting

It is essential to collect samples properly. Collect only what you absolutely need for your collection. You also should not collect in such a way that you damage landscape or scenery or might cause a landslide or cave-in.

Remember to be careful to follow rules and regulations on public lands. Most national and many state parks, including state beaches in some states (for example, California), prohibit the removal of any natural material from their grounds. Therefore, remove specimens from public land only after you have determined that such collecting

Figure 8 Geologic specimens can be found
almost anywhere. In the foreground
of this scene in Bronx, New York,
are pieces of mica schist.

is allowed. A good guide to follow in off limits places is: "Leave only footprints, take only pictures."

It is absolutely necessary that you ask permission from the owner of the land before you enter private property. Most landowners or companies are very helpful. Make sure you tell them why you wish to go on their land, and be sure to abide by any restrictions or safety regulations they impose. A letter or note from a teacher or parent explaining the purpose of your project may be helpful.

Talking to Other Collectors

One of the best ways to learn about rocks and minerals and where to find them is to talk to other collectors. You will find them everywhere, sometimes in the most unlikely places. Ask at school or home. Talk to teachers, to friends and their parents, people at rock shops, naturalists at nature centers, and members of gem clubs. *Lapidary Journal* in its April issue publishes a national list of about 1,000 such clubs, and there's bound to be one near you or in your state. Such clubs often have shows (also listed in the magazine), to which you can bring your own specimens for comparison. You're bound to "turn over" a rock hound or gem hunter where you live. The magazine also lists conventions, shows, dealers, and other information.

If there is no club in your area, consider starting your own. You will probably lure many active and occasional rock hounds and gem enthusiasts out of the woodwork.

Safety

When you go collecting, be sure to notify or take along a responsible adult. Always take an adult when you are visiting a potentially hazardous area such as an excavation, road cut, or quarry. When collecting, wear appropriate clothing (including long-sleeved shirts, long pants, and a hat), sunscreen, safety goggles, and gloves. In a quarry, *wear a hard hat.*

The Tools of the Collector

When you go on a collecting trip, you will want to take along a collecting bag for specimens, tags and labels (or white tape); a pen, marking pen, or pencil; a hammer and chisel or rock hammer; safety goggles or a face shield; your notebook; local maps; and field guides. You also may want to take a watch, compass, camera, small tape recorder (on which to record observations and notes), sketching or casting materials, plastic bags and vials for specimens, and tissue paper to wrap fragile specimens.

Labeling and Cataloging Specimens

The key to collecting for a science project is to carefully record information about specimens when you find them. If you pick up a rock and shove it into your bag, you will never remember where or when you found it. And if you don't identify it either in the field or once you return home, there's a good chance you will simply end up with a pile of rocks that you will never get around to doing anything with.

Therefore, when you go collecting, carefully record the general location you are working in your notebook or on your tape recorder. You might want to take photographs as well, or make sketches. Note the date and, if you have a map, the spot on the map. (U.S. Geological Survey maps show the location of quarries.)

Tag or label the specimens themselves at the site with the date and place of collection. Place larger specimens in bags; smaller specimens, such as sand, dirt, mineral flakes, and tiny pebbles can go in a vial. Record other information about the specimen, too, including the location (for example, "top layer of syncline"). Numbering samples is also an excellent idea. Samples can then be referenced by number in your notebook, and you will have much more room to describe them—and an easier time writing than on small labels. Drawings of the site can be made directly in the field book, or photos can be attached to the pages.

In other words, make as many notes about the sample and the collecting site as you can. You can identify the specimens later.

How to Choose Specimens
The best rock or mineral samples are roughly rectangular and have at least one fresh surface. **When you are breaking, sledging, or trimming specimens, be sure to protect your eyes from flying pieces of rock with safety goggles or, ideally, with a special plastic shield.** Take a look again at Figure 3 in Chapter 1. Wrap trimmed specimens in newspaper or tissue and label them.

What Specimens to Collect
Figure 9 shows some of the specimens you may collect:

• Minerals—substances (usually inorganic, i.e., lacking in carbon) with a definite chemical composition and set of physical properties, such as hardness, density, etc. Examples are quartz, pyrite, olivine, mica, and feldspar.

• Ores—substances composed of a combination of minerals from which metals can be extracted. Examples are hematite, galena, and gold.

• Rocks—substances composed of one or more minerals. One example is granite, which is composed of feldspar, quartz, and other minerals (one of which is often mica).

• Gems—minerals of a very high grade, valued for their beauty or durability. Examples are diamonds, emeralds, and amethysts.

• Fossils—rocks that contain traces of organisms that lived a long time ago.

Your collection can be diverse and include all of these types of samples, or it can contain just one type.

Figure 9 A selection of specimens:
(a) granite (rock), (b) amethyst (mineral),
(c) garnet (gem), (d) hematite (ore),
and (e) a fossil

Identifying Your Specimens

Now that you have collected some samples, you will want to identify them. Compare your samples with pictures and descriptions of samples in rock and mineral identification books (listed in the For Further Reading section at the back of this book). Identifying minerals is difficult, so don't expect to be able to identify them all. You may want to get help from a teacher, local geologist, or experienced rock collector.

Displaying Your Specimens

Set up a display of your samples at your home or maybe a traveling display that you can take to school. Other people may enjoy looking at your interesting collection. Of course, an exhibit can be part of a science project for a classroom assignment or science fair, but to compete for a prize you probably will have to do something more than just arrange a display. Extensive information on displays can be found in the two books mentioned earlier in this chapter.

INVESTIGATING THE PHYSICAL PROPERTIES OF ROCKS AND MINERALS

In order to identify and classify the samples in your collection, it is important to determine some of the physical properties of the samples. Physical properties are those properties that do not change just because you break the sample into smaller pieces. Some important physical properties are specific gravity, density, hardness, heat capacity, reflectivity, conductivity, and ferromagnetism. In the next series of projects you will have an opportunity to determine some of the physical properties of your samples.

Calculating Specific Gravity

Specific gravity is the ratio of the mass of a given volume of a substance to the mass of another substance used as a standard. Water has been chosen to be a standard substance in measuring the specific gravity of liquids and solids because it is common and easy to work with. Knowing the specific gravity of your specimens will greatly help in their identification, since many field guides and other books describing minerals list the specific gravity of each item.

MATERIALS

A balance, samples of rocks or minerals, thread, and containers of water.

PROCEDURE

Use the balance to measure the mass of a sample in air. The units you use to measure the mass are not important, as long as you use the same units all the time. Attach the thread to the sample and measure the mass again while the sample is suspended in a container of water, making sure to keep the sample from touching the sides of the container. The type of balance you have may require some ingenuity on your part. Refer to Figure 10.

Now you can calculate the specific gravity of the sample, using the following method. Subtract the mass of the displaced water from the mass of the dry sample. Then divide this difference into the mass of the dry sample. The result is the specific gravity. Below is an example of the calculations.

Step 1. Subtraction

	mass of sample in air	70.0 g
−	mass of sample in water	50.0 g
=	loss of mass in water	20.0 g

Step 2. Division

$$\text{specific gravity} = \frac{\text{mass of sample in air}}{\text{loss of mass in water}} = \frac{70.0 \text{ g}}{20.0 \text{ g}} = 3.5$$

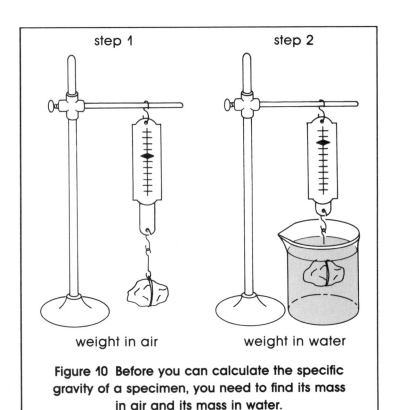

step 1   step 2

weight in air   weight in water

Figure 10 Before you can calculate the specific gravity of a specimen, you need to find its mass in air and its mass in water.

Repeat this procedure for each of the samples in your collection. List them in order of increasing specific gravity. This list will prove helpful in identifying and classifying your samples.

Calculating Density

Specific gravity and density are related. They both show the relationship of the mass of an object and its volume. You can guess the density of a rock simply by palming different specimens of similar or even different sizes. For instance, some small rocks feel much heavier than some very large rocks. The small rocks have more mass per volume. Some volcanic ash is amazingly light. You may be able to lift huge boulders of volcanic ash with one hand simply because they aren't very dense: they contain very little matter per unit volume. Quantitative measurements of density can be useful in helping you to identify your specimens.

One way to calculate density is to find the mass of a specimen, measure the volume of water displaced by the specimen, and divide the mass by the volume. Try this on a few of the samples whose specific gravity you have already calculated and compare the figures.

Is one method easier than the other? Is one method a better way to identify rocks and minerals? Can you find a better way to measure density?

Other Projects with Specific Gravity and Density

With a little experience, you can learn to estimate the specific gravity of rocks by how heavy they feel. The "heft" of a sample is often a useful field test.

• If you think you have any meteorites in your collection, determine their density and specific gravity and their scientific names. Check against data you find on comets, asteroids, meteor showers, planets, and moons. Do you think your specimens came from any known sources?

• Would you expect minerals with a high specific gravity to be hard or soft?

• Can the different types of rocks—igneous, metamorphic, and sedimentary—be typed by density and specific gravity?

• Do specimens with high densities also have high specific gravities?

• Working backward from data you find on the density and specific gravity of rocks from the moon and from Mars, can you predict what the surface of some bodies in space would be like to walk or ride on? Would special shoes or tires be needed?

• Compare the specific gravity of your samples with the average density of the Earth that you calculated in Chapter 2. What do you find? What do you think the interior of the Earth is made of? Design an accurate model that illustrates what you find.

• Some rocks float. Try to find one that does. How could you determine the specific gravity of a rock that floats?

Measuring Hardness
Another characteristic of minerals and rocks is hardness. Hardness is the measure of a substance's ability to abrade, scratch, or indent another substance. Most scales of hardness are relative scales; that is, they indicate the hardness of one substance relative to another. In this project, you will devise your own scale of relative hardness.

MATERIALS
Safety goggles, rock and mineral samples, a hardened steel punch, a plastic tube 20 inches (50 cm) long and large enough in diameter for the punch to fit into, a calibrated loupe (available from a photography supply store), and a 10-power hand lens.

PROCEDURE
Put on the safety goggles. Be careful of flying pieces of rock. Find a flat spot on one of the samples. Hold the tube above the flat spot, and drop the punch through the tube so it strikes the sample. Make certain you always drop the punch from the same height so that the force of the punch on the samples is always the same. Make three punch marks on each sample.

Now examine the punch marks very carefully with the

hand lens. Exact measurements of the marks are possible using the calibrated loupe. Record the diameter and depth of the marks with a ruler or calipers. Are the size and depth of the marks related to the hardness of the sample? Arrange your samples in order according to the size or depth of the punch marks. Do the harder samples have larger impressions or smaller ones? Does the punch go deeper into softer or harder ores? Perhaps a ratio of size and depth would be a good way to estimate the hardness of the sample.

Compare your figures with those in books. Can you identify your samples using hardness and specific gravity and density? Which property is easiest to use for identification? The most universal hardness scale that geologists use is Mohs' scale, shown in Figure 11 with some simple tests. How does it compare with your scale?

Determining Heat Capacity

Heat capacity is a measure of how easily a material can be heated or cooled. Heat capacity of rocks can be determined by heating samples to 212°F (100°C) in boiling water, then transferring them to water at room temperature. Measure the rise in temperature caused in the water by the samples as they lose their heat to the water.

Determine the heat capacity of some of the rocks or minerals in your collection.

Does specimen size affect heat capacity? Does the above method of measuring heat capacity take into account factors such as size, shape, and quality? If it doesn't, see if you can modify the technique to improve the results you get.

• Is there any connection between heat capacity and density, specific gravity, and hardness?

• What other factors would influence the loss or gain of heat in your experiment?

Figure 11 Mohs' hardness scale with some common field tests

Hardness	Index Mineral	Field Test
1	talc	Sample will not scratch fingernail.
2	gypsum	Sample will barely scratch fingernail.
3	calcite	Copper penny just barely scratches sample.
4	fluorite	Steel scratches sample easily.
5	apatite	Steel barely scratches sample.
6	feldspar (orthoclase)	Steel does not scratch sample. Sample scratches window glass.
7	quartz	Scratches all glass and steel easily. This is the hardest common mineral.
8	topaz	Scratches quartz. This is a rare mineral.
9	corundum	Scratches topaz and all common minerals. This mineral is used in abrasives.
10	diamond	Hardest of all minerals. Quite rare.

For Further Investigation

• Rocks are often used in solar-energy heat-storage systems. Would any of the rocks in your collection work well in such a system? If you aren't happy with the rocks you already have, make a special search for the best local rocks for such a purpose.

• Design a storage system using the rocks you have collected. Is it possible that a variety of rocks, arranged in layers, would work better than one layer of one type of rock?

• Is a rock solar-heating system superior to a plain water-storage system? How good is a combination rock-and-water system?

• Investigate more fully the concepts of heat capacity, specific heat, and heat transfer; then study maps of the geologic structure of the area you live in. Can you make any predictions about the presence of volcanic activity such as hot springs or underwater sources of hot water? Does the nature of the rock in your area affect the weather? Could you make a "temperature map" of your area, both above ground and below ground? Check your map against thermal contour maps produced by satellites.

Measuring Reflectivity

Some rocks are shiny; some are dull. Reflectivity is a measure of how much light is reflected off a material compared with how much is shining on it. Experiment with your samples to find out how they reflect light. (A photography light meter may be helpful.) Then construct a scale that "reflects" your findings.

• Does a weathered surface of a rock reflect light differently than a fresh cut or a broken surface?

• Can you make any generalizations about the reason some rocks and minerals are shinier than others?

• Are there any fixed correspondences between reflectivity and other properties of your samples?

• Where do transparent or partly transparent samples fit on your scale?

• Is there a practical or financial value to a mineral's reflectivity? If you don't have any gold, silver, or precious or semiprecious gems in your collection, try to do some research at a local museum or in conjunction with a club or private collector. Does shininess have anything to do with the value of gold, platinum, and silver? Investigate some of the applications of rocks and minerals based on their reflectivity.

Measuring Conductivity
Thermal conductivity is a measure of how well heat flows through a material. It is an important property used by geologists to determine the nature, structure, and composition of the rocks under the surface. Figure out a method to measure the rate of heat flow through your samples. Then research the rate of heat flow of various rocks in your area.

• Rocks, concrete, and bricks are often used as building materials. Why would the thermal conductivity of a material be important in determining its appropriateness as a building material?

• R-value is a measure of the insulating property used in the building industry. How does R-value relate to thermal conductivity? What is the R-value of various building materials?

• At geothermal areas, heat from hot materials from below the Earth's surface is transferred to rocks and groundwater at or near the surface. How would the thermal conductivity of the materials affect this transfer?

Investigating Ferromagnetism

Are any of your rocks or minerals magnetic? Do you have any lodestones in your collection? Do any of your samples react to a magnet? Investigate your collection for magnetic properties. A good way to do this is with a compass or with a small magnet suspended by a string. Also do some reading about natural magnetism, starting with descriptions of the discoveries of the ancient Greek philosopher-scientist Thales.

• How do you suppose natural magnets got the way they are?

• Do natural magnets have the same properties as artificial magnets and electromagnets? Do some systematic comparisons of natural and artificial magnets to test your ideas.

• Investigate theories regarding the origins of the Earth's magnetic field.

• Try making a compass the way the first compass makers did, using a magnetic rock.

• Investigate the supposed ability of some organisms to detect the magnetic lines of force around the earth and to navigate by using this ability. Don't forget magnetobacteria, bacteria that are "magnetic."

• Do you have any meteorites in your collection? Are they magnetic? Do some research on meteors and meteorites, perhaps visiting a science or nature museum with meteorites in its collection. If you are very ambitious, you could investigate the magnetic properties of moon or Mars rocks, either in a research paper or experimental project.

• You could do a project tracing the development of our knowledge about magnetism, from lodestones to superconducting magnets. Why is magnetism so important in science and technology?

• Next time you are at the beach, collect some sand and test it for magnetic properties. For example, see what happens if you run a magnet through some sand. If your results are in the affirmative, find out why. Could it be something in the water?

CLASSIFYING ROCKS AND MINERALS

Geologists deal with the tremendous variety of Earth materials by sorting them according to various classifications, of which the two most common are type (rocks and minerals) and origin (igneous, sedimentary, and metamorphic). Who is to say, however, that these or other standard systems are the best way for you to classify the specimens in your collection?

You can in fact develop your own classification system for your collection, using all of the information you have gained about the physical properties of your samples. However, the important thing to remember when setting up any classification system is that it be consistent, practical, and reproducible; that is, someone else should be able to classify the samples in the same fashion.

You might start out separating by color. For example, separate out all the white samples. Then classify the white samples by specific gravity or hardness and so on. Further classify the white stones by different levels of hardness. And so on and so forth. This is your classification system, and as long as you can use it to understand and learn more about the materials that make up the Earth, it is a good system.

• Is the system you devised also used by geologists? If not, why not?

•   Is your system useful in helping you identify the samples by their accepted scientific names?

•   Although the current classification systems have been in use for many years, there is no reason why a better system couldn't be devised that scientists eventually might adopt. Although the art of scientific classification is not in vogue today the way it was in the past, some scientists do pursue this traditional and important branch of science. Perhaps you can devise a new, complete, and better classification system for rocks, minerals, and other Earth materials.

4

MAKING AND STUDYING CRYSTALS

If you have ever taken a close look at a diamond or other precious stone, then you will probably have at least some appreciation of the beauty and structure of crystals. Other crystals are more mundane but no less remarkable and fascinating. Even salt or sugar crystals viewed under a microscope reveal a structure at once symmetrical and intriguing, as you can see from Figure 12.

What exactly are crystals? How do they get the way they are? Why should nature build a material from identically shaped pieces? What happens when you smash a crystal to bits? Do the individual bits exhibit the same shape as the unbroken crystal? Is there a point beyond which the crystalline structure of material disappears?

Geologists are interested in crystals because they tell them about the internal structure of the mineral. By observing the crystal shape, the geologist can determine the arrangement of the atoms or molecules that make up the crystal. Studying crystals was one of the first ways scientists learned about atoms and how they are arranged.

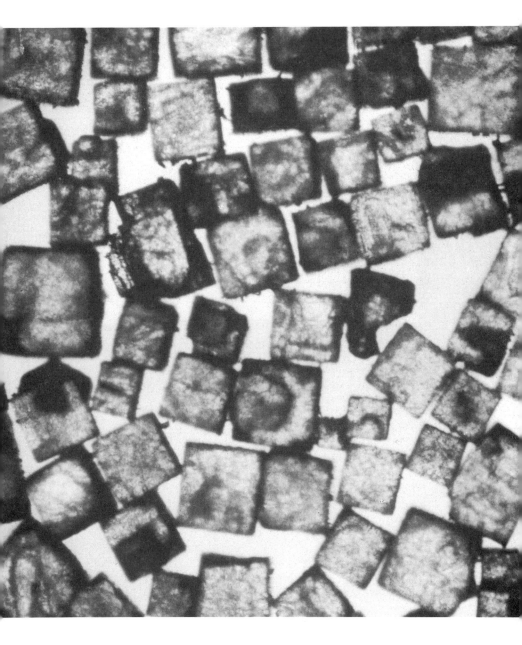

Figure 12 Salt crystals, magnified ten times

You can investigate crystals both in the laboratory and in the field. Using either way, you are sure to come away with a new-found appreciation and understanding of crystals.

Safety Note. Many of the lab projects in this chapter require the use of chemicals and flames, so be sure to:

• **wear approved safety goggles, as well as protective gloves and a lab apron if necessary**

• **work in a well-ventilated area**

• **have safety equipment such as fire extinguishers and fire blankets handy**

• **work only under the supervision of a knowledgeable adult such as a science teacher**

• **when heating a test tube, point it away from your face and eyes and away from other students**

• **wash your hands after each project**

MAKING SULFUR CRYSTALS

Most rocks crystallize directly from magma, or molten rock. As the magma cools, its atoms form an ordered arrangement called a crystalline structure. You can simulate this process in the laboratory.

MATERIALS

Approved safety goggles, a lab apron, protective gloves, a Pyrex test tube [18 millimeters (mm) X 150 mm], 15 g powdered sulfur, filter paper, a 500-milliliter (mL) beaker, a wire test-tube holder, a candle, a hammer, and a magnifying lens or microscope.

PROCEDURE

1. Put on the safety goggles, lab apron, and protective gloves.

2. Fill the test tube about halfway with the powdered sulfur.

3. Fold the filter paper in half and then in half a second time. Open one of the folds so that the filter paper forms a cone. Place the open cone in the beaker.

4. Using the wire test-tube holder, hold the test tube over the lit candle. Heat the test tube evenly by constantly moving it in the flame. The melting sulfur will turn dark yellow as it melts. **Be careful not to overheat the test tube, to prevent the sulfur from catching on fire.**

5. When the sulfur appears completely melted, pour it into the paper cone. Allow the sulfur to cool for a few minutes.

6. Break the filter cone by lightly striking the cone with the hammer.

OBSERVATIONS
Carefully observe and note what you find in the filter paper. Study the crystals using the magnifying glass or microscope. Record the size, shape, color, and angles of the crystals. Make a detailed drawing of the crystals.

EXPERIMENTS AND QUESTIONS
Read about crystallography and the different forms of crystals. Compare the sulfur crystals with the various forms.

• Break off a small piece of the crystals. Compare your observations of it with those you made of the whole piece. Are there any similarities or differences?

• After allowing the crystals to stand for several days, make the same observations and answer the same questions as you did above. Are there similarities or differences? If so, why?

• Perform the experiment again to check the validity of your answers.

• Melt another sample of sulfur as you did before. The sulfur must be heated to near its boiling point, and it will turn a dark-red color. It may be necessary to use a gas burner to supply more heat. This time, however, **slowly and carefully** pour the molten sulfur *directly* into a Pyrex beaker containing cold water. What happens? Could the resulting material be an amorphous substance?

Safety Note. Be sure to use the burner under adult supervision and in a lab where safety equipment is available. Light the burner very carefully, since the flame is hot and dangerous. Keep the flame away from flammable materials. Extinguish the flame and turn off the gas completely when not in use.

• If you have any sulfur crystals in your collection, compare them with the ones you made and take note of and explain the differences and similarities in chemical and physical properties. Construct a display around the crystals from different sources.

• Working under supervision, substitute sulfur you find in nature for the commercial sulfur you used in the above experiments. Compare your results.

For Further Investigation
• Investigate the nature and uses of sulfur, trying to answer such questions as why sulfur is yellow, why it forms crystals, and whether all sulfur is crystalline.

• Sulfur is usually mined using a procedure called the Frasch process, which takes advantage of the very low melting point of sulfur (261°F or 113°C). Research this process and make a scale model of a sulfur recovery operation.

MAKING OTHER CRYSTALS FROM MOLTEN MATERIAL

Experiment as you did above but with paraffin, mothballs, salol, and water. Ask your teacher to suggest other substances or chemicals as well. **When heating mothballs, do so in a well-ventilated area, ideally in a fume hood.**

MAKING CRYSTALS FROM SATURATED SOLUTIONS

If you were to walk along the edge of the Great Salt Lake, in Utah, you would see deposits of white crystals on the beach, as shown in Figure 13. These crystals are composed of various substances but mainly sodium chloride, the same ingredient as in most table salt. The crystals were formed when the water evaporated. Before they formed, they were dissolved in the water, forming a solution.

Many rocks and minerals are formed in this way, sometimes in huge quantities, both naturally and artificially. In this project you will dissolve crystals in water and then evaporate the water to form crystals.

Safety Note. Handle the chemicals in this project carefully and work only under the supervision of a qualified adult.

MATERIALS
Approved safety goggles, a lab apron, and protective gloves, labels, pencil or pen, six glass dropper bottles (15–25 mL), distilled water, a balance, a metal pan, an

**Figure 13 Salt deposits along the
Great Salt Lake in Utah**

electric hot plate, tongs or an insulated glove, six micro-scope slides, a 10-power hand lens, two electric light sources (for example, spotlights), and the following chemicals:

- 4.0 g of sodium chloride (NaCl)
  5.2 g of sodium bromate ($NaBrO_3$)
  2.4 g of aluminum potassium sulfate ($KAl (SO_4)_2 \cdot 12H_2O$)
  9.3 g of potassium ferricyanide ($K_3Fe(CN)_6$)
  6.2 g of copper(II) sulfate hydrate ($CuSO_4 \cdot 5H_2O$)

PROCEDURE

1. Put on the safety goggles, lab apron, and protective gloves.

2. Label each dropper bottle with the name of one of the substances listed above. Fill each dropper bottle with exactly 10 mL of distilled water. Use the balance to mea-sure the required amounts of each substance, and add the substance to the bottle so labeled.

3. Place the metal pan on the hot plate and fill the pan with distilled water to a depth of 2.5 cm.

4. Increase the temperature of the hot plate to just be-low the boiling point of water.

5. Place the dropper bottles in the hot water.

6. Using tongs or an insulated glove, shake the bottles occasionally to dissolve as much of the solid as possible.

7. When the substances have pretty much dissolved, place 1 to 3 drops of each solution on its own microscope slide. Make sure none of the solid at the bottom of the bottle gets into the liquid.
   If you spill any of these chemicals on yourself, wash it off with water.

EXPERIMENTS AND QUESTIONS

• Use the hand lens to observe the drops as they cool, illuminating them with one of the spotlights. Do they form crystals? Record your observations. If nothing is happening, hold the other spotlight over the solution to speed up the crystallization process.

• Describe the similarities and differences among the crystals. Are any the same shape? Classify the crystals by their geometric shapes.

• Make detailed drawings of the crystals.

• If you have the equipment, photograph or videotape the process of crystal formation of the resulting crystals. You may need special lenses or adapters to work through a microscope. The resulting photos or tapes would make a nice science project display in themselves or a valuable visual aid to a project on crystals.

• Try growing crystals in darkness, in different-colored light, in polarized light, or in ultraviolet light. You can grow the crystals in a homemade container with different lights, filters, etc.

• Perform the experiment again but under different conditions. Try tap or spring water, heatproof bottles of different size or shape or made of other materials, or a different heating or cooling rate. Try working in a darkened room, a room with a colored light, or an air-conditioned room. Try "natural" evaporation or more or less of the chemical. Try working "at an angle" or "upside down." Record your observations and explain what you see.

FOR FURTHER INVESTIGATION

• Research natural and artificial crystal formation by evaporation and compare these processes with the process you have just used. Can you improve on established artificial processes? Can you predict the kinds of crystals that will be found under different types of natural evaporation processes? Can such processes take place underground?

• Collect and examine salt crystals that have formed on rocks near the ocean or by other sources of saline water. Also see if you can check out the salt produced by commercial desalinization facilities, or desalinize your own salt water. Many questions can be asked about such salt, and many experiments done.

• Study kosher salt, rock salt for cooking and making ice cream, rock salt used on icy surfaces, and other commercial varieties of salt. Do a project on the history of salt, which at one time was more valuable than gold.

MAKING CRYSTALS FROM MORE THAN ONE SOLUTION

Make crystals using a mixture of two or more of the solutions from the previous project, "Making Crystals from Saturated Solutions." **Do not mix any solutions other than the ones listed.** What do you observe? Do you suppose this is the process involved in the formation of some rocks? Find similar crystals in nature and compare them with the ones you have made.

MAKING MODELS OF CRYSTALS

Most minerals can be classified as one of the six basic systems illustrated in Figure 14. These systems are based on the angles between the axes. Research these systems and determine whether your crystals fit these categories. Identify these shapes in the crystals that you have made. Then make some large styrofoam or wooden models of the shapes. A good project could combine models with the real thing, along with details of your comparison studies,

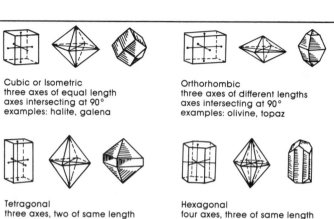

Cubic or Isometric
three axes of equal length
axes intersecting at 90°
examples: halite, galena

Orthorhombic
three axes of different lengths
axes intersecting at 90°
examples: olivine, topaz

Tetragonal
three axes, two of same length
axes intersecting at 90°
examples: chalcopyrite, cassiterite

Hexagonal
four axes, three of same length
three axes intersecting at 60°
examples: quartz, apatite

Monoclinic
three axes of different lengths
two axes intersecting at 90°
examples: gypsum, kaolinite

Triclinic
three axes of different lengths
no axes intersecting at 90°
examples: albite, labradorite

Figure 14 The six basic crystal systems

drawings and photographs, and perhaps even computer-generated models.

If you are not convinced that models can be high-level projects, do some reading on the work of Linus Pauling, who won a Nobel Prize for his work on the nature of the chemical bond, and on Francis Crick and James Watson, who shared a Nobel Prize for the discovery of the structure of the DNA molecule. A model of a section of a DNA molecule is shown in Figure 15.

GROWING LARGE CRYSTALS

Quite often, natural geologic forces conspire to produce large crystals. If you have ever seen a precious stone such

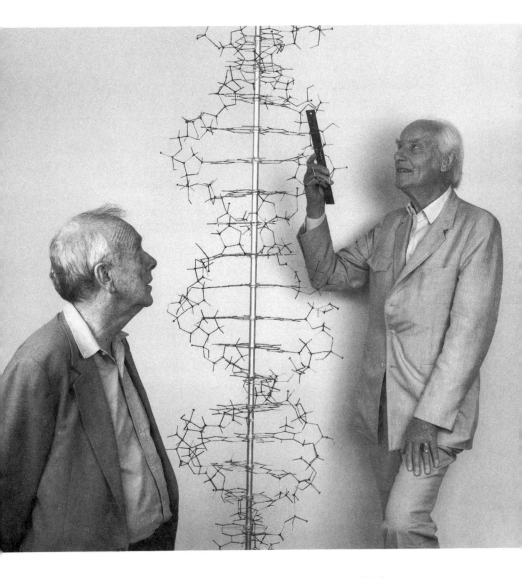

Figure 15 Francis Crick (right) and James Watson,
who discovered the helical structure
of the DNA molecule, are standing next
to a model of part of it. Models are
extremely useful in scientific work.

as a diamond, then you already have seen such a crystal. Although large crystals aren't always gems, quite often they are. Sometimes these crystals are not just large; they are *very* large. Mineral collectors prize such crystals because they are rare and often quite beautiful.

The formation of such crystals requires special conditions, as you will learn in this project to grow a large crystal directly from a solution.

Growing a Large Alum Crystal

To grow a large crystal of alum, you first will grow a seed crystal. The seed crystal is necessary to provide a surface for the large crystal to grow from.

MATERIALS

Safety goggles, a lab apron, protective gloves, a 100-mL graduated cylinder, a 250-mL Pyrex beaker, distilled water, a balance, 100 g of alum [potassium aluminum sulfate dodecahydrate (KAl $(SO_4)_2 \cdot 12H_2O$)], an electric hot plate, tongs or an insulated glove, thread, and a pencil or paper clip.

PROCEDURE

1. Put on the safety goggles, lab apron, and protective gloves.

2. To make a seed crystal, measure 200 mL of the distilled water into the beaker and add 48 g of the alum. Place the beaker on the hot plate and heat until all of the alum is dissolved. Do not boil the solution! Turn off the burner and remove the beaker **with the tongs or insulated glove** and place it on a hot pad.

3. Allow the solution to cool to room temperature. Then drop in a few crystals of the alum.

4. Set the beaker in a place where it won't be disturbed and leave it for several days.

5. Examine the solutions. You should see several crystals about 1/4 inch (6 mm) long. These will be your seed crystals.

6. Remove one of the seed crystals from the beaker and attach a piece of thread about 20 inches (50 cm) long with a slip knot. Set the crystal aside.

7. Reheat the solution on the hot plate until the alum is again dissolved. Turn off the burner.

8. Tie the thread to a pencil or straightened paper clip suspended across the top of the beaker, as shown in Figure 16, so that the crystal is suspended in the solution. Let the solution cool as you did before. Do not attempt to speed up the cooling process. Just let the solution cool at room conditions.

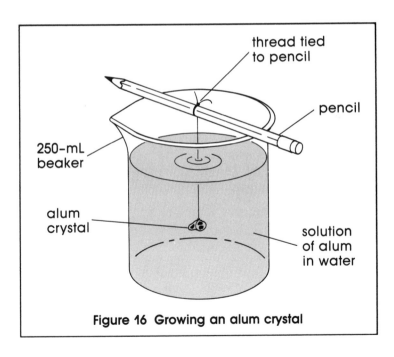

Figure 16 Growing an alum crystal

9. Leave the solution undisturbed for several days.

10. Remove the seed crystal from the solution. Then add another 8 g of alum and reheat on the hot plate to dissolve the new alum.

11. Repeat step 8.

12. Repeat the above procedure until you have a large crystal.

EXPERIMENTS AND QUESTIONS
• Examine the crystal closely, with and without a hand lens. Describe its color, hardness, shape, etc. Is it "perfect" or flawed? Draw or photograph the crystal. Read up on alum and on this kind of crystal. Do you have any similar crystals in your rock and mineral collection? Are such crystals found in nature? If so, how are they formed? If not, why not?

• Repeat the experiment several times and see if you can grow a bigger or better crystal.

• Change some of the conditions—for example, the type of water, amount of water, amount of alum, type of alum, cooling and heating time, etc. Deduce some rules for growing crystals.

• Can you grow a double crystal with two seeds? A triple crystal? Are alum crystals always the same shape and color? Try to produce alum crystals that are different.

• Photograph or videotape the growing crystal. Is growth regular, or does it vary in the experiment with the time of day, amount of light, temperature and humidity, etc.?

• Try growing the crystal in a cold or hot place, for instance, the refrigerator or on a radiator or in sunlight.

Growing Large Crystals of Other Substances
Grow large crystals using other substances, such as table

salt, sugar, and epsom salts. Make certain that the substances used are not toxic or explosive. Check with an adult before proceeding.

Compare these crystals with those of alum. Compare procedures, conditions, and results. Then explain the differences and similarities.

For Further Investigation

•   Do some research on large crystals and prepare a display incorporating what you find with the giant crystal or crystals you grew, your observations about growing crystals, and possibly some large (or smaller) crystals you have in your collection. You might want to include models, drawings, and photographs.

•   What happens when you break a large crystal? Try breaking a crystal by striking it gently with a hammer. **Be sure to wear safety goggles and to watch out for pieces of flying crystal.** Experiment with different types of fractures. Do crystals of different sizes have the same properties except for size?

•   Investigate the occurrence of large crystals in nature.

•   Look into crystal formation in caves, around hot springs, and in other exotic areas. **Be sure to work under adult supervision.**

•   Check out geodes and mineral crystals such as quartz and amethyst. These can often be found in rock and gift shops.

•   Photograph (after obtaining permission) large crystals at museums and jewelry and gift stores. The results will be both beautiful and instructive.

BUILDING A GONIOMETER

A goniometer is a device used to measure the angles crystal faces form with one another. Instructions for building such a device can be found in some mineralogy books or can be obtained from mineral experts. Use the finished instrument to study the crystals you have grown as well as any crystals you have in your collection. What kinds of conclusions can you draw from your investigations?

• What happens when a crystal is broken down to the smallest possible size? Can scientists measure the angles of the individuals atoms in crystals? If so, what do you think they would find? Check up on your answer.

GROWING CRYSTALS IN SPACE

Figure 17 consists of two photographs: one of crystals grown on Earth, the other of crystals grown in space. Which do you think is which?

What kind of crystal would you expect to grow in space? Would it be bigger and better than on Earth, or smaller and less regular? What would be the effect of low gravity on shape, size, color, hardness, and quality? In Figure 17, the space-grown crystals are on top. They are not bigger than their earth-grown counterparts, but they are "more ideally shaped." In this case, the ideal shape is a square bipyramid. The crystals are made of a protein from the venom of a cottonmouth snake. Interestingly, the ideal shape wasn't known until the crystals were grown in space.

Astronauts *have* grown crystals on Skylab and on the space shuttle. Investigate these efforts. Can you simulate space conditions in your lab and grow "space" crystals of your own? If it's possible to test your predictions, what do you find? See Bruce Smith and David McKay's *Space Science Projects for Young Scientists* (New York: Franklin Watts, 1986) for more information.

• Find out whether there are crystals on the moon, in meteorites, or on Mars. If so, do they resemble those found on Earth? Would they be formed in the same way?

Figure 17 Earth-grown and space-grown samples of
the same crystal. Which is which? (See text for answer.)

• Compare your findings about space-grown crystals with your findings about Earth-grown crystals. Are the conclusions consistent?

• Would a space-based crystal factory be financially successful? Design your own facility for growing crystals, for use either in space or on the moon or Mars. Don't forget to include a system for returning the crystals to Earth.

USING CRYSTALS IN SCIENCE AND TECHNOLOGY

Research applications in science and technology for crystals. For example, calcite was used during World War II in bomb sights (do you know why?), garnet is used in sandpaper, and gem-quality minerals are obviously used in jewelry. Construct a display that includes descriptions of such applications along with sample crystals and the information you have gathered on crystal structure and formation. Find out why particular crystals are used for special purposes.

• Is there a difference between natural and synthetic diamonds? Do they have any similarities? How are they the same? Why are natural diamonds usually more valuable than synthetic ones?

5

HOW OLD
IS THE EARTH?

How old is the Earth, and how old are its features? You can read the answers in books, but the ages you find will probably be so large they have no meaning for you. To get an idea of the concept of geologic time and the huge numbers involved, think about some of the people and events in your own life.

If you are in junior or senior high school, you were born about 11 to 17 years ago. Your parents, then, were born perhaps 30 to 60 years ago, before humans landed on the moon, possibly even before World War II. Your grandparents were born between 40 and 100 years ago, so one of them could conceivably have been born before the turn of the century, before the electric light was invented. Your house or apartment is probably from one to 100 years old, and depending on where you live, your town could have been first settled up to 300 years ago. Local museums might contain art created 800 years ago, nearby Indian ruins could be still older, and artifacts in museums from ancient civilizations could be 3,000 or 4,000 years old. If you were to go back to the beginning of human history—that is, recorded history—you would go back not much farther.

By contrast, the dinosaurs became extinct about 70 *million* years ago, and the oldest geologic features in North America were formed about 2 *billion* (2,000,000,000) years ago. The Earth itself is thought to be almost 5 billion years old.

Such huge amounts of time measured by geologic events are referred to as *deep time*. Geologists must develop techniques to determine and express such huge and unfathomable amounts of time.

Geologists divide geologic time into eras and periods as shown in Figure 18. Unlike familiar units such as hours, days, weeks, and years, such geologic time units are of varying length. For example, a period may be as long as 70 million years or as short as 2 million years. The beginning and end of such time units are marked by significant events—for instance, the disappearance of the dinosaurs—rather then a specific passage of time. It is like saying that individual days end when you happen to go to bed, rather than at a specific time.

TIME IS ON THE LINE

Time lines can form the basis of one or more interesting science projects. You can begin by designing a simple time line whose geologic eras are represented by sections of proportional length. For example, have 1 inch or 1 cm equal 1 million years. Do this by hand or, if you are handy with computers, on a computer.

• Draw a large-scale time line on a long roll of paper or cloth or perhaps on a more permanent material (like concrete) in a public place. Be sure to obtain permission. This time line could be filled in with words and drawings. You could elaborate your time line with photographs and specimens. The result would be a kind of environmental

Figure 18 The geologic time scale and some significant events it spans.

Era	Period	Millions of Years Ago (Beginning)	Significant Events
Cenozoic	Quaternary	2	Most recent ice age begins and ends.
	Tertiary	65	Major mountain ranges rise (Rockies, Alps, Himalayas).
Mesozoic	Cretaceous	136	Dinosaurs become extinct.
	Jurassic	190	Pangea begins to break up; Mediterranean Sea begins to form; dinosaurs common.
	Triassic	225	Age of Dinosaurs begins.
Paleozoic	Permian	280	Pangea forms; many life forms become extinct.
	Pennsylvanian	320	Appalachian Mountains rise; coal swamps form.
	Mississippian	345	Early amphibians appear.
	Devonian	395	Early Atlantic Ocean begins to close.
	Silurian	430	Early shellfish begin to leave sea.
	Ordovician	500	First fish and land plants appear.
	Cambrian	570	Oxygen content in atmosphere increases; marine invertebrates become common.
Proterozoic		2,500	Simple life forms develop.
Archeozoic		4,600	Planet evolves from cosmic debris.

science art. The time line could become a community project or part of a fair or festival. Use water-soluble chalk unless the project is to be permanent. When you are done with the line, walk down the line noting the position of the various events. As you do, think of the vast amounts of time that each of your steps is consuming. It stretches the imagination!

A Local Time Line

Did you ever wonder about the geologic history of your neighborhood, why certain rocks are there, or why rocks there are arranged in a certain fashion? Make a time line of the geologic history of where you live. Fill it in with details depicting what it was like in the past. Can you predict the future geology of your neighborhood?

• Collect specimens made by humans (new and old—for example, jars) and natural specimens (for example, rocks, sand, bones), date them, and display them with your time line. Photographs or drawings could be used in addition to, or instead of, actual specimens.

• Determine the age of the rocks in your area by researching the studies which have been done about the geology in your neighborhood. Find a rock outcrop and be able to say "That rock is so many years old."

Pictures of the Past

Photographs like those in Figure 19 show what happens to some areas over time, in this case as a result of human intervention. Using old photographs, compare the way features in your area like mountains, hills, valleys, or other geologic features looked in the past with the way they look now. Are there any differences? If so, were the changes caused by humans or by nature? Take your own pictures so that you can prepare a comparative photo exhibit. As part of your exhibit you could bring in specimens showing changes caused by forces such as erosion.

Figure 19 Above: Hetch Hetchy in Yosemite before
the dam was built. Below: Hetch Hetchy
flooded after the dam was in place.

• How long do you think it would take to change these features beyond recognition? For example, if a small stream has deepened a small canyon, how long would it take to cut a channel hundreds or thousands of feet deep?

• Make a working model that simulates the changes taking place in the geologic features you are studying.

FOLLOWING THE PAPER TRAIL

Geologists are often concerned less with the exact time of an event than with its relative time, that is, its occurrence in reference to that of other events. For example, the end of the Cretaceous period is usually marked by the extinction of many species of dinosaurs. Although the exact time in years of this event may change as new information is found, its position relative to other events will not.

In this project you will simulate, in a personal way, one of the methods geologists use to reconstruct geologic history based on the deposits left behind.

MATERIALS

A cardboard box 3 to 6 feet X 1 1/2 feet X 1 1/2 feet (1 to 2 m X 0.5 m X 0.5 m), a piece of plywood the same size as the inside of the box, several bricks, and a ruler.

PROCEDURE

Place the box someplace—at home or school—convenient for people to deposit their waste paper (newspapers, notebook paper, magazines, etc.). Make a sign instructing people to throw all such paper—but not food waste, liquids, or other nonpaper products—into the box.

Keep track of the first day of the project. At the end of each day, place the piece of plywood on top of the pile and put the bricks on top. Measure the height of the papers at regular intervals, for example, daily or weekly. Make a scale drawing of the pile in your notebook and mark the times on the drawing.

QUESTIONS

Try to answer the following questions about the pile: Where are the newest and oldest papers located? On the average, at what rate does paper accumulate? Is the rate of accumulation uniform?

PROCEDURE

Now remove about ten pieces of paper from various positions in the pile and set them aside. You will come back to them after the following part of the project.

Let the paper accumulate at least a month; then begin excavating the paper piles starting from the top. As you proceed, selectively record the actual date (if it is available), time, depth, and nature of significant events, for example, birthday parties, deadlines for class projects, obituaries, election results, doctors' appointments. When you are through, mark the events on the drawing in your notebook.

FOLLOW-UP

You now have what is called a geologic column of the pile of papers, a sequential inventory of the recorded events and deposits. From this you could create your own geologic calendar using significant events to mark the time units. Use the geologic time scale as a model.

Now retrieve the ten pieces of paper you previously set aside. Using the geologic column you just constructed, can you determine the "age" of each paper?

You could, if you wish, continue this project over a longer period, for instance, a semester. If you do this, be sure to analyze the contents of the box constantly or you will wind up with a roomful of trash!

THE ROCKY TRAIL TO THE PAST

Excavate (with permission) a column of geologic material in your neighborhood and use the above-described method to determine the sequence of geologic events.

DATING AND MEASURING SNOWFALLS

If you live in an area where it snows, carefully excavate a small section of snow late in winter. Choose a flat place like your backyard or a flat spot in a small local park. **Under no circumstances should you do this project on or near a hill or mountain or in the woods, since you may trigger an avalanche or be exposed to avalanche danger. (An avalanche can sweep down a hill, through wooded areas, and across a flat area too.)** Can you date the major snowfalls? Can you determine the amount of each snowfall? Hint: See what happens if you melt the snow and examine the microscopic particles in the snow.

POLLEN DATING

Investigate dating methods using pollen. One student, for example, studied the lead content in pollen and found out the date that automobiles using leaded gasoline were first used in her area.

INVESTIGATING FOSSILS

Start a collection of fossils, ideally of local origin. Investigate different dating methods and try using them on your specimens. Can the geologic column method be used?

• Investigate how fossils are formed and try to re-create these processes. Compare your homemade fossils with the real ones from a museum or other collection. What differences, if any, are there?

HUNTING DINOSAURS

Did dinosaurs ever live near where you live? What evidence was used to determine whether or not they did? Study artifacts such as dinosaur footprints. How can these be proved to be real?

- Many popular comic strips or cartoons, such as "B.C.," "The Flintstones," "The Far Side," and "The Last Dinosaur," use geologic history in their stories. Investigate these strips for accuracy. If you are not happy with what you find, either "fix" the mistakes or create your own, scientifically accurate comic strip or cartoon.

MEASURING ABSOLUTE TIME

Often it is important for geologists to determine the exact date of a particular event. This is called *absolute time*. In order to measure absolute time you must be able to measure the occurrence of some event which occurs at a very predictable rate. For instance, a watch uses the regular vibrations of a quartz crystal or the oscillations of a pendulum to measure exact time.

To measure geologic time, geologists need some regular event which occurs at a predictable, reproducible rate over extremely long periods of time. The rate at which certain radioactive atoms decay into more stable atoms is a very predictable event. Can you think of an event that occurs at a predictable, very stable rate? Design a method or device for measuring time which uses such an event. (An hourglass is one such device.) Remember that the event must repeat or change over a predictable time period.

HOW OLD IS THE EARTH?

Despite limitations, cooling rates, erosion rates, and other rates can be very useful in determining the absolute time of various events. Estimates of the time of geologic events can be made by knowing the rate at which sediments are deposited, erosion occurs, or glaciers move.

An early scientist, Lord William Thomas Kelvin, used the rate at which the molten Earth cooled to its present state to estimate the age of the Earth. His estimate, made in the late nineteenth century, put a maximum age on the Earth of about 100 million years. We now know that the Earth is much older than that. Kelvin made a major omission in his assumptions about the cooling of the Earth. Research the work of Lord Kelvin and see if you can determine the omission he made.

• Present methods of determining the age of the Earth involve measuring the rate of decay of radioactive isotopes. Research the methods scientists use to determine the age of materials 5,000 years old, 1 million years old, and 1 billion years old.

• Carbon-14 dating is used by archaeologists to determine the age of human artifacts. Find out why carbon-14 is not useful to find out the age of very old rocks such as those over 3 billion years old which have been found in Canada.

• Go to a university or a museum and observe how radioactive decay is used to determine the age of materials. Perhaps you could arrange to have an object of yours dated.

Investigate the processes that created the Grand Canyon (Figure 20) and find out if they are at work on a smaller scale, perhaps even in your neighborhood or region.

RADON

Radon is a gaseous element which is the product of natural decay of the uranium in rocks. Recently you may have heard a lot about the possible contamination of homes in various parts of the United States.

Do some readings on the problem, its causes, and the effects of radiation on human beings, plants, animals, viruses, and other organisms. Also read up on radioactive decay, background radiation, and cosmic rays.

Then use a radon-detector kit or geiger counter to

Figure 20 The Grand Canyon is one of the most
spectacular places on earth and a geologic
laboratory for peering into the past.

find out whether radon gas is present in your house or in other buildings in your area. What types of geologic formations contain or produce radon? Are there other sources of radioactivity in your surroundings, for example, "background radiation"? If you live in a big city, pay a visit to large public buildings like train stations and scan them for radiation. What do you find?

Make a contour map showing the distribution of background and other radiation sources that exist in your community. Be sure to include any reactors, storage areas for radioactive materials (in hospitals, for example), or other facilities. Always obtain permission before you do your investigations.

6

EARTHQUAKES
AND VOLCANOES

Two major geologic events that occurred in the United States in the 1980s reminded us that although we would like to think of the Earth as a stable, predictable place to live on, in fact it is not so stable and not so predictable after all.

Do you recognize Figure 21? It shows Mount St. Helens in Washington State violently erupting in 1980, showering ash on the surrounding countryside, destroying trees and other vegetation and killing several people. And what about Figure 22? That shows some of the havoc wreaked in 1989 when a major earthquake struck San Francisco, damaging buildings, highways, and bridges, starting fires, and killing scores of people.

In a day when it seems as if we have almost limitless control over our landscape—after all, we can dam mighty rivers, cut down mountains, and build huge lakes—we still cannot accurately predict the weather (let alone earthquakes and volcanic eruptions) nor can we control or prevent these natural phenomena. All we can really do at present is try to understand the causes of earthquakes and

Figure 21 Mount St. Helens erupting

Figure 22 Damage from the 1989 San Francisco earthquake

volcanoes and try to predict their behavior in order to protect human lives and minimize the economic impact.

In the simplest terms, a volcano is a vent in the Earth's crust through which rock and hot gases erupt. This mixture of rock and hot gases works its way up from beneath the Earth through weaknesses in the crust.

An earthquake is an oscillation of the Earth's crust as a result of the movement of two pieces of the Earth's crust past each other along fractures. These fractures, called faults, represent weak points in the crust. The faults may be horizontal or vertical. During an earthquake, energy spreads from the center of the quake (called the focus) and rapidly radiates in all directions. The point on the surface of the Earth directly above the focus is called the epicenter. It's the vibrational energy that sways and cracks roads and houses and that you feel as a shaking or a jolt. Figure 23 shows the San Andreas fault in California.

MODEL OF A FAULT

You can build a working model of a portion of the Earth's crust to simulate earthquakes. Building and using this model will allow you to learn some things about the cause and effects of earthquakes—even though the model is obviously on a much smaller scale than the Earth.

MATERIALS

A roll of 1-inch masking tape, two pieces 1/4-inch-thick plywood about 12 inches X 24 inches, moist sand, toothpicks, plaster of paris, and a 35mm camera (optional).

PROCEDURE

Working on a flat surface, tape the boards together as shown in Figure 24. Push on the boards so that they move in opposite directions, as shown. Note how the tape is deformed. Keep applying pressure. What happens?

Figure 23 A section of the San Andreas fault
in San Luis Obispo County, California.
Imagine what a city built on or
near the fault would look like,
and you may better understand
the previous photograph.

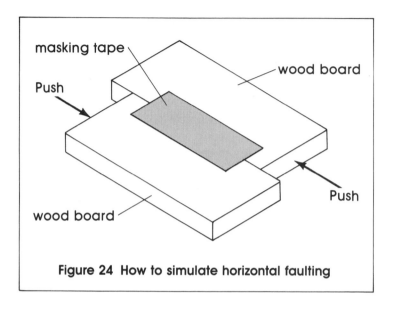

Figure 24 How to simulate horizontal faulting

Repeat the experiment, but this time cover the boards and tape with moist sand about 1 inch (2–3 cm) deep. Place several rows of toothpicks in the sand across the fault. Move the boards slowly as before and observe carefully what happens. What happens to the toothpicks? If you have a camera, photograph the formation of the fault. How could you measure how far one block has moved with respect to the other block?

• Investigate different types of faults and earthquakes and try to simulate them with this or other simple models. What type of faulting were you able to observe in the first experiment?

For Further Investigation
• Study local faults, if there are any, and reports of earthquake activity along them.

• Compare what you can learn about faults and quakes from simple models, with what scientists actually know about faults and quakes. Modify your models if your results are not satisfying. For a science fair project you could combine the models and simulations with information you gather from books and scientists and from direct study of faults and quakes.

Faulting Ups and Downs
You can use the same materials to investigate vertical faulting. Place the two boards so they are about 4 inches (10 cm) apart. Now cover the boards and the empty area between the boards with sand. Push the boards toward each other. What happens? Keep pushing the boards toward and even over each other. What do you observe? Describe the faults that occur. Photograph the different steps of the process.

Do Different Materials Fault Differently?
Using the same methods described above for simulating faults, put a thin layer of plaster of paris on the sand and let it dry before performing the experiment. Also try modeling clay, gelatin, corn starch, or other materials. Carefully keep track of the results.

• Now see if you can transfer what you have learned to a study of real faults, faulting processes, and earthquakes. Focus on the area you live in. If you have done some of the earlier projects in which you studied the structure and composition of the crust in your locale, you will have a good start in this project.

Lubricating the Fault
Some scientists believe that lubricating faults—by injecting water into them—may prevent major earthquakes. Try this

with your model and investigate thoroughly the research in this field. What are the advantages and disadvantages of water as a lubricant? Would other fluids work better? Which ones? Test them on your model.

Earthquakes and Buildings

Build a small model city on your model and simulate the faulting and earthquakes. Document what happens to the buildings and other structures. Experiment with earthquake-proof designs to find the strongest materials and the best building techniques. Try "floating" tall buildings on water or other fluids to see what happens. Is this done with real buildings?

• Study reports of real earthquakes around the world to learn more about the effects of quakes on buildings and cities. Can any building designs save cities from the "really big ones"? Are some cities more earthquakeproof than others? Design a model earthquakeproof city and test your ideas.

BAD VIBRATIONS

Much of the major damage caused in the 1989 San Francisco earthquake resulted from strong vibrations, which caused failures in the materials that buildings were built on. When strongly shook, some earth materials will become quite weak and will act like a liquid. This process is called liquefaction. Using the fault model you built, you can test various materials for their ability to liquify.

Spread wet sand over the fault area. Take a small hammer and gently but rapidly strike the wooden board from the side. Observe the reaction of the sand as it vibrates. Try different materials and various rates of vibration. Perhaps you could design a motorized vibrator to cause continuous shaking. Put buildings on the surface and experiment with various kinds of structures and see which ones hold up the best. In making these buildings, make certain they are made of materials heavy enough to sink into the surface. Good materials to use would be bricks, pieces of metals, or rocks.

MEASURING THE SHAKING

Figure 25 shows a seismograph, a device used to record the magnitude and length of an earthquake (and other types of Earth movements). A network of seismographs is in place connecting different seismic stations around the world. The basic principle of a seismograph can be illustrated by hanging a heavy object like a brick or a rock from a chair. Use a thin, but strong piece of twine to hang the object so that it hangs just above the floor. Gently shake the chair. Notice the object doesn't move very much. This is how seismologists, scientists who study earthquakes, measure Earth movement.

See if you can design a model seismograph that demonstrates how a real seismograph works. If you are more ambitious, look in books or articles for more sophisticated designs. Or design a real seismograph of your own.

Visiting a Seismic Station
Visit a local seismic station and find out how the seismograph detects and records Earth movements and how sensitive it is. While you are at the station, you should be able to get a lot of information on earthquakes in your state. Make a list of dates and magnitudes and see if you can detect a pattern. If possible, test your ideas.

How Large Is an Earthquake?
Seismologists measure earthquake magnitude either by how much energy the earthquake releases or by how much damage is caused. The two scales used for this are the

Figure 25 This geophysicist points to the trace
of an earthquake on a seismograph.

Richter scale and the Mercalli scale. Research both of these scales. A good science project might be to list the major earthquakes which have occurred in the world and make a large chart comparing their Richter scale values and their Mercalli ranking. Can you design a more accurate scale?

BUILDING AN ERUPTING VOLCANO

A volcanic eruption often causes earthquakes, explosions, and lava flows. Predicting volcanic eruptions, though a fledgling art, is an important aspect of the work of volcanologists—scientists who study volcanoes—and many geologists.

Since you may not live near either an active or dormant volcano and may lack access to other sites of volcanic activity such as geothermal vents, hot springs, or geysers, an excellent way to learn more about volcanoes and volcanic activity is to build your own volcano.

MATERIALS
A balloon, a rubber band, a piece of rubber tubing with an outer diameter of 1/2 inch (13 mm), a plastic pan about 4 inches X 24 inches X 24 inches, sand, toothpicks, about a pint of plaster of paris, water, and a 35mm camera (optional).

PROCEDURE
Referring to Figure 26, attach the (deflated) balloon to the tubing with the rubber band. Make sure you don't close off the rubber tubing. Put the balloon on the bottom of the plastic pan and cover it with sand at least 3 inches (8 cm) deep. The balloon represents a magma chamber beneath the surface of the Earth. Prior to erupting, molten rock often collects in a large reservoir called a magma chamber. Smooth the surface of the sand.

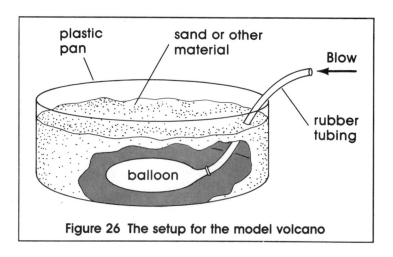

Figure 26 The setup for the model volcano

QUESTIONS AND OBSERVATIONS

Slowly inflate the balloon by blowing into the tubing. Observe the surface of the sand very carefully. Continue inflating the balloon. What happens? Allow air to escape from the balloon.

Can you translate what you have learned to "real" geology? What could you measure that would indicate that the chamber below a volcano was filling with magma? What observations could you make that would indicate that a magma chamber was emptying in a real volcano?

Detecting the Bulge

What happens beneath a volcano just before it erupts? To find out, smooth out the sand and arrange in it the toothpicks over the area you think the volcano will erupt. Make sure the toothpicks stick straight up. Inflate the balloon very slowly. What happens? Does a real volcano do the same thing?

Can Volcanoes Be Controlled?

Is it feasible to control volcanoes? Use your model to find a way to prevent eruptions. What modifications if any would be needed to prevent eruptions of a real volcano? Would a different method be needed on different types of volcanoes, for instance, shield volcanoes (for example, Mauna Loa, in Hawaii) and cone volcanoes (for example, Mount St. Helens)?

Changing the Surface Materials
Repeat the above series of experiments using wet or damp sand. You could also make layers of sand and plaster of paris and then inflate the balloon.

What types of patterns form when the more solid crust is pushed aside?

Compare your patterns to those formed by real volcanoes or regions of the Earth where large magma chambers are forcing the Earth's crust apart. Try to re-create the events which produce such features and record them with a camera.

Changing the Erupting Materials
What happens when the erupting materials are changed? Instead of using air for magma and a balloon for the magma chamber, try forcing a mixture of sand and water into a balloonless area under some sand to see what happens when you cause an "eruption." You may need a lot of pressure to force the sand through the tube. You might get some ideas from talking to a contractor who does "mud jacking" to raise heavy pieces of concrete using mud.

VOLCANIC MATERIALS

Molten rock that flows from a volcano or other opening is called lava. Lava cools and hardens into different types of rocks. The type of rock depends on what minerals are in the lava, how fast they cool, and whether hot gases are present.

Research some of the volcanic materials and artifacts shown in Figure 27, as well as other materials. Determine

**Figure 27 An assortment of volcanic materials:
(a) obsidian, (b) "bread crust bomb,"
(c) tuff, (d) snowflake obsidian, (e) ash, and (f) pumice**

how these materials were formed and what uses they have.
Develop a display of commercial uses of volcanic materials. You might wish to expand this into a display of other
commercially useful rock materials.

7

PLATE
TECTONICS

Take a look at Figure 28. Now imagine the continents closed up. Do they fit together? A look at Figure 29 may lead you to answer with a resounding yes!

The German scientist Alfred Wegener made the same observation over eighty years ago and concluded that the continents were joined at one time and had since drifted apart to their present positions. At the time his ideas were thought to be absurd, but eventually he collected enough data to support his hypothesis. Today scientists have evidence that the continents did move and in fact are still moving.

The theory that explains continental drift is now called plate tectonics. It says the surface of the Earth is made up of large plates that are constantly moving. Plate tectonics theory helps us understand how continents and oceans form, why and where earthquakes occur, and why volcanic eruptions take place. Figure 30 shows a map of the positions of the tectonic plates. Several projects in this chapter investigate correspondences between the positions of these plates and the location of such features as

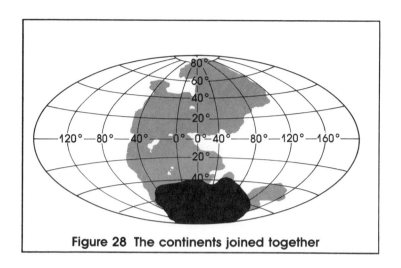

Figure 28 The continents joined together

volcanoes, mountains, and rivers and of such phenomena as earthquakes.

DRIFTING CONTINENTS

To further explore the idea of drifting continents, you will need a large map of the world that not only shows the landmasses but also the ocean floor features such as the continental shelf and the mid-oceanic rifts.

Glue the map to a piece of cardboard. Cut out the major landmasses from the map, following the continental margin as defined by the continental shelf. Then try to fit the pieces together in different ways. What do you discover?

Now assemble the continents to make the best fit possible. What would you expect to find if you studied the rocks on the edges of the continents? In other words, if South America and Africa were once one continent, what would be true about the rocks where the continents were in contact?

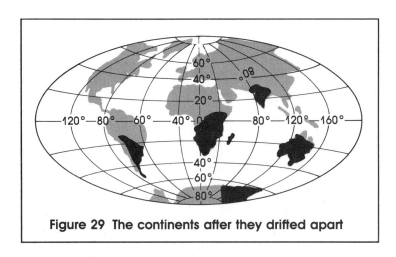

Figure 29 The continents after they drifted apart

Can you find evidence to support your hypothesis? And conversely, does the geologic evidence—age of the rocks, distribution of fossils, age and distribution of undersea rocks, etc.—point to your arrangement of the continents? Assemble the data on the map pieces.

If your evidence does not support one arrangement of continents, try another one. How does your arrangement compare with Wegener's or with more contemporary arrangements?

For Further Investigation

• If you are very ambitious and have a lot of time, develop pen pals in some of the key areas you think once fitted together and exchange samples. You would then have a truly global science project, similar to the projects international teams of scientists sometimes conduct.

• Research the development of our ideas about the positions of the continents, beginning with the ancient geographers, philosophers, and scientists. Did any of the ancients get it right?

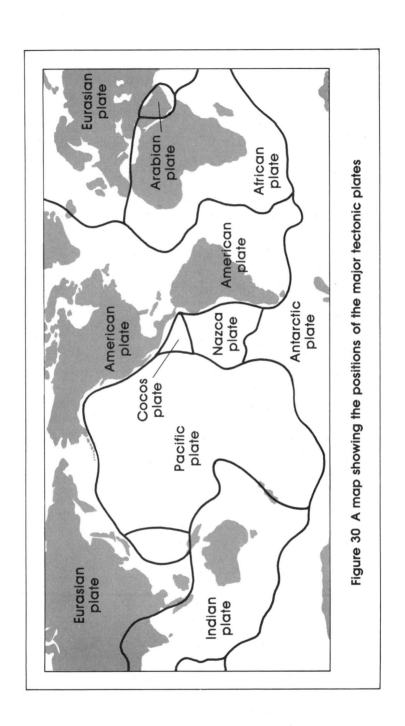

Figure 30 A map showing the positions of the major tectonic plates

•   Do the map project using a globe. Use tape or Velcro to reattach the continents to a second globe that you have built. Explain any differences in results.

Drifting into the Future
Do some research to find out the speed and direction of continental drift and use that information to predict where the continents will be at various times in the future. Arrange your map or globe to reflect the position at these times, and photograph or draw the arrangements. If you are handy with a computer, you could write a graphic simulation to show the entire spectrum of the drift, from way in the past to way in the future.

Drifting into the Past
Were all the continents part of one landmass? If so, was there an arrangement before that landmass?

PLATE TECTONICS—A MODEL OF EARTH MOVEMENT

You can build a model to show how scientists believe the tectonic plates move toward, away, and past one another. With this model you can demonstrate the formation of mountain ranges, volcanoes, and earthquakes.

In the model you will use cardboard to represent the asthenosphere (the layer below the Earth's crust), paper strip to represent the oceanic crust, wood or clay blocks to represent the continental crust, and tissue paper to represent sediments. The first simulation will be of the collision of the Indian plate with the Eurasian plate.

MATERIALS
    A scissors or knife, a ruler, one piece of cardboard 12 inches X 20 inches (30 cm X 50 cm), a roll of calculator paper at least 3 inches (8 cm) wide, two pieces of modeling clay (or wood blocks) about 2 inches X 4 inches X 4

inches (5 cm X 10 cm X 10 cm), tissue paper of two or three different colors, masking tape, hairpins, and a physiographic map of the world.

PROCEDURE

1. Cut two slots in the cardboard as shown in Figure 31.

2. Cut two lengths of the calculator paper at least 30 inches (75 cm) long.

3. Form the pieces of clay into blocks the same width as the calculator paper and about 2 inches (5 cm) high. You could use wood blocks instead of the clay.

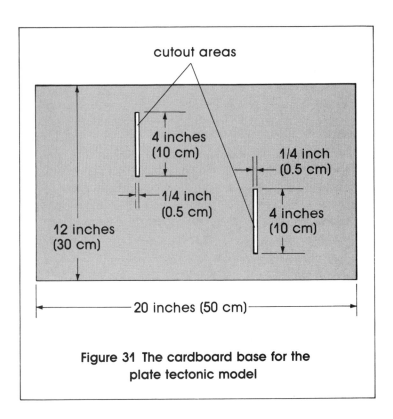

Figure 31 The cardboard base for the plate tectonic model

4. Cut the tissue paper into strips as wide as the calculator paper.

5. Using the masking tape if necessary, attach one block of clay to the cardboard at the edge of the slit (Figure 32).

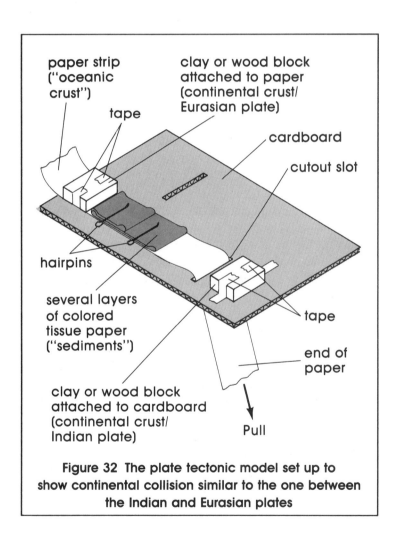

Figure 32 The plate tectonic model set up to show continental collision similar to the one between the Indian and Eurasian plates

6. Attach the other block of clay to the end of the piece of calculator paper (Figure 32).

7. Thread the other end of the calculator paper through one of the slots in the cardboard until the clay end just reaches the end of the cardboard (Figure 32).

8. Use hairpins to attach two or three layers of tissue paper to the calculator paper in the space between the two pieces of clay (Figure 32).

USING THE MODEL

You are now ready to use your model to build mountains. Pull on the calculator paper coming out of the bottom of the cardboard so that the clay moves toward the slot. Continue to pull slowly until no further movement is possible. What happens when you pull?

What you have just done simulates what happens when two continental masses collide due to convergent plate movement. The collision causes the trapped layers of sediments and sedimentary rock to fold, bend, fault, and generally be metamorphosed and uplifted. Orogeny, or mountain building, is the result. This is similar to what happened when the Indian plate carrying a piece of continental crust collided with the Eurasian plate approximately 40 million years ago. Find this area on the world map. Figure 30 may be of help too.

Now do some research to learn more about the other types of plate movements. Then use the model and a little imagination to simulate these movements. Locate the places on the map where these movements are occurring.

MODIFYING THE MODEL

Modify the model to make it more closely approximate the movements of the real tectonic plates. Since a model is only as good as its parts, you may, for example, need to learn more about the behavior of rocks in order to come up with better model rocks.

Local Plate Tectonics

•   Do some research on the plates under your city and on the various major rock formations, mountains, faults, sites of volcanic activity, volcanic artifacts, etc., where you live. If you are lucky enough—or unlucky enough—to live in the San Francisco Bay area, you may learn something very interesting about the plates in this area, for example.

•   Do a project on the tectonic history of your area and make predictions about the future. Take photographs, make drawings, write computer simulations, collect specimens, study the age of the formations, investigate phenomena like "earthquake lights," etc.

•   Make a working model showing the plate action "under your feet."

MAGNETISM AND
PLATE TECTONICS

Much of the recent research in earth science has been directed toward understanding more fully the exact nature of the movement of the plates on the surface of the Earth. Information has come from a wide variety of scientific disciplines, including geophysics, biology, oceanography, and archaeology. One of the most interesting avenues of research has been on magnetism.

Some rocks contain molecules that act like tiny magnets. When the rock is molten, these magnets can float in the rock and arrange themselves with the magnetic field of the Earth. (To illustrate this phenomenon, place a small magnet on a small toy boat. Observe how the boat orients itself; then turn the boat and observe its movement.) When these rocks solidified long ago, the molecules "froze" in place, recording the direction of the magnetic field on Earth at the time.

Use iron filings, plaster, and a large magnet to try to simulate the formation of such a rock. How can you now detect the orientation of the filings in the plaster?

For Further Investigation
• What would happen if the magnetic field of the Earth changed direction—that is, north became south and south became north? Or what would happen if the position of the magnetic poles changed? Would this affect the orientation of the magnetic molecules or of the iron filings? Find out if such reversals have indeed occurred, and if so, try to modify your model accordingly.

• Could a polar reversal occur today or in your lifetime? If so, how would our lives be changed? Imagine you are a scientist or engineer designing a master magnetic plan for the world. What would you do to deal with these changes? For example, would you have to change all the world's maps and compasses and other scientific instruments that depend on magnetism?

• Could a knowledge of magnetic molecules and terrestrial magnetism be used to better understand the movement of the plates? Are plates magnetic? Entire continents?

• Do other planets or moons have magnetic fields? Do these fields work the same as the Earth's?

• Many scientists believe that the Pacific Ocean was created by the impact of an asteroid. Others believe it possible that the ocean fills a crater left by a large chunk of matter pulled out by the sun to form the moon. What evidence—magnetic or otherwise—is there for these hypotheses? Can you model them to see which one seems more likely? Any ideas of your own?

EVOLUTION AND PLATE TECTONICS

What would happen if a species of animal lived on a continent that eventually broke apart? Would the populations evolve differently?

• Research the evolution of elephants to find out whether the two living species of elephants—Indian and African— are an example of such an occurrence? What about mammoths?

• Look into the development of other species, for example, camels and horses. Where did they originate? Plot the locations of related species on a world map.

• Read up on Charles Darwin and how he developed his hypothesis for the origin and evolution of species through natural selection. Are there any current examples of species development similar to those on which Darwin developed his hypothesis? Do these have any connection with our beliefs about the drifting continents?

THE PLOT THICKENS

Plot the locations of the tectonic plates (Figure 30), major faults, earthquake epicenters, and major volcanoes on a world map. Is there a relationship between the locations of the boundaries of plates and the other features? Why is it that the rim of the Pacific Ocean is often called the Ring of Fire?

8

HYDROGEOLOGY

It's in your body, in your food, in the air. It's in the sky, on the ground, and under the ground. It runs, falls, and flows, freezes, boils, and evaporates. It sits peacefully, slowly wears, swiftly cuts. What is it? If you guessed water, then you would be right.

In one form or another, water has been part of our planet for billions of years. Over that time it has helped shape the features of the Earth, from mountains to valleys. Rain washes away soil from gardens, and a mighty river carved the Grand Canyon. Life began in water, and to this day all living things, from microbes to human beings to whales, need or rely on water. Human beings, for example, are about 90 percent water.

Water is constantly eroding the Earth. The force of moving water—as rain, snow, hail, ice, steam, streams, rivers, and oceans—wears away sand, soil, and rock, and also erodes human-made creations such as roofs, foundations, pipes, and automobiles. Eroding water sometimes carries away what it erodes, as happens when a stream or river carries away dirt as it swells during a heavy rain. A glacier may—ever-so-slowly—push ahead of it even huge boulders.

It is this eroding action, on a large scale and over a long time, which has worn away mountains, dug canyons, built up deltas at the mouths of rivers, and in numerous other ways shaped the features of the Earth. Although the results of such erosion are often beautiful—as you can see in the photograph of the Grand Canyon shown in Chapter 5 (Figure 20)—sometimes the results are not so beautiful. For example, a flood can kill people and can destroy homes, roads, and other buildings, as you can see illustrated in Figure 33.

BUILDING AND USING A STREAM TABLE

A stream table is a model of an actual river. Water erosion can be observed under controlled conditions in a stream table, a small-scale model of a river that you can build without too much trouble. Remember that models, although useful, do not represent the "real thing" in all aspects.

MATERIALS FOR STEPS 1–3

A sturdy table at least 2 feet × 7 feet (0.6 m × 2 m), six pieces of wood 2 inches × 4 inches × 18 inches, a screwdriver, four small hinges, a water source such as a faucet or hose, two pieces of wood 2 inches × 4 inches × 20 inches, scissors or knife, one piece of heavy cardboard 2 feet × 5 feet (0.6 m × 1.5 m), twenty 1-inch aluminum roofing nails, and heavy-duty polyethylene film 3 feet × 6 feet (1 m × 2 m). Note. Metric measurements are not used for some materials because they usually are not sold that way.

MATERIALS FOR STEPS 4 AND 5

Small wood scraps or blocks, two pieces of hose ¼ inch × 5 feet (6–7 mm × 1.5 m), electric drill with ¼-inch bit, metal tubing ¼ inch × 2 inches (6–7 mm × 5 cm), bathroom caulk, two pinch clamps, about 50 pounds (23 kg)

Figure 33 A flooded town on the Mississippi River

of clean sand, a small recirculating pump (optional), very large container to collect runoff.

OTHER MATERIALS
    A video camera (optional).

PROCEDURE
    Refer to Figures 34 and 35 while following these directions.

1. Start by building the frame shown in Figure 34. The frame should have three sections that move relative to one another.

2. Cut the cardboard into three sections and attach them with the nails to the bottom of each section. Trim off any excess cardboard. Turn the frame over so the cardboard is on the bottom. Place two pieces of loose cardboard on the inside of the frame to cover the gaps between the cardboard pieces, but do not attach these. See Figure 35.

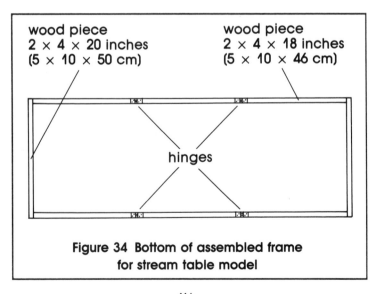

**Figure 34 Bottom of assembled frame
for stream table model**

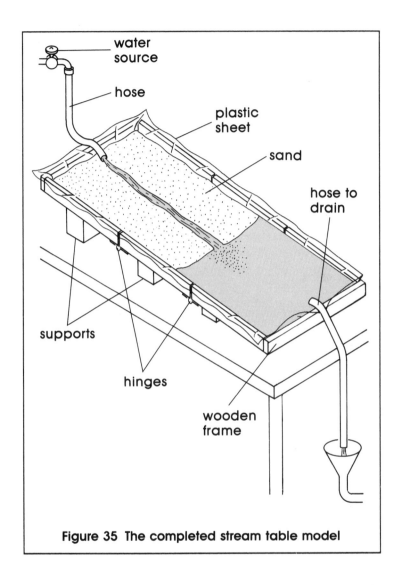

Figure 35 The completed stream table model

3. Line the inside of the frame with the polyethylene film.

4. Using the small wood scraps or blocks, raise one end of the stream table about 2 inches (5 cm). The middle of the table should be about 1 inch (2–3 cm) above the ta-

ble. This will create a slope for the water. Pour the sand in the stream table and spread it over the top two-thirds.

5. Connect one of the hoses to the water source. Attach the hose to the upper end of the stream table. As the water collects at the bottom of the stream table, the water must be removed. This can be accomplished in one of several ways: (1) Drill a hole in the end of the frame. Push the metal tubing through the hole and pierce the polyethylene liner. Seal the gap around the tubing with bathroom caulk to prevent leakage. Attach the rubber hose to the tubing with the clamps and drain it into a sink or floor drain. (2) Siphon the water out. (3) Use a small recirculating pump.

In order to prevent sand particles from getting into and clogging drain systems, it is a good idea to have the water drain into a large settling tank. Then draw the water off the top of the tank into a drain.

Now that you have built your stream table, you are ready for some experiments.

Is There an Erosion Cycle?
What exactly happens during water erosion? Is the process always the same?

To find out, make a straight channel ½ inch (1–2 cm) deep in the sand along the length of the stream table. Create a heavy flow of water and note what and how fast things happen. Repeat this procedure several times. Are the results the same?

Now vary the flow of water. Compare what happens, and compare how fast things happen.

What can you conclude about the effects of water erosion on an existing channel?

Now vary the slope of the stream by raising or lowering sections of the stream table. Observe carefully what happens.

If you have a video camera, tape the different "runs" of the experiment.

• Explore the area you live in, or any parks or forests you go to on trips, to see if you can find examples of erosion that resemble those you observed with your stream table. Take photographs and collect samples of rocks, sand, and dirt. Can you find small-scale evidence of water erosion on the samples? If you live near a stream or river, can you document the effects of water erosion over a period of several months or a year?

• If the erosion you see in nature is somewhat different from that occurring in the stream table, can you modify the stream table setup or procedure to more closely simulate the effects?

Making a Canyon
Use the stream table, sand, and pebbles or small rocks to create such processes as differential weathering, slumping, and landslides as well as such features as canyons, waterfalls, and rapids. Can you accomplish these things in different ways, or is there one way only? Are there different types of canyons?

• Find examples in nature of these features and processes and compare them with those you have simulated. You might be able to take a close-up photo or video of a stream table waterfall that looks very much like a real waterfall.

Rivers and Towns
Many cities and towns are built near or on rivers. New Orleans is on the Mississippi, Albuquerque is on the Rio Grande, Paris is on the Seine, London on the Thames, Moscow on the Volga, and so on.

Although many benefits accrue from such proximity, there are disadvantages as well, as you saw in Figure 33. Often, in fact, cities can be at the mercy of their rivers, even in our modern age.

Form a medium-size river in your stream table and build

a town or city near or on its banks. You might want to model your city and river after ones you know or research.

Now vary the flow of water to see what happens. If there is flooding, you may need to design some fortifications. In extreme cases, you may need to do some major work on the river itself.

• Do some research on a river city that has existed a very long time, for example, Rome. Study the changes in the city and river made over the years to deal with erosion, flooding, etc. See if you can predict the future look of such a city, based on your knowledge of the erosion and flooding caused by the river.

• Some people actually live on the flood plains of rivers. What happens during high water? Is there any way to combat the effects of the water, especially during the spring, when flooding may occur?

Building a Dam
Construct a dam across a stream table river that allows you to control the water level above the dam and the flow coming out of the dam. Construct a movable gate system. How can large boats get past the dam?

It's Raining, It's Pouring
Use a showerhead or similar attachment to simulate the effects of rain on different surfaces.

• Investigate the effects of real rain on natural features and on synthetic materials. Compare your findings with findings from the stream table experiment.

THE ACTION OF WATER ON COASTLINES

It is said that the eccentric billionaire Howard Hughes once bought property in Tucson, Arizona, because he thought it would one day be shoreline property—after California and part of Arizona fell into the Pacific Ocean. Although the whole of California will not fall into the sea, its coastline is constantly changing, and in places, cliffs and beaches are eroding away.

Coastline erosion by the ocean as well as by storms, rising sea levels, artificial structures, slides, and earthquakes occurs on all coastlines, not just those in California. The shifting fortunes of the sea have altered the shape of Cape Cod, in Massachusetts, for example, ever since it was settled by the Pilgrims. Sometimes we seem to ask for destruction of our houses by building them too close to the water when we know the water can be destructive. Other times our efforts to stem erosion end up making the situation worse. For example, sea walls intended to protect structures often destroy beaches by diverting the waves' energy to more unmanageable areas. Have you ever seen coastal erosion like that shown in Figure 36?

Building a Model Beach

You can investigate shoreline erosion using a model sand beach. If you live near a beach, you will want to make some field studies as well.

MATERIALS

5 pounds (2 kg) of fine silica sand, a disposable aluminum cake pan 15½ inches × 10½ inches × 2 inches, water, various objects to produce waves, a small quantity of aquarium gravel, and various objects (plastic blocks, stones, pebbles, etc.) with which to construct jetties, breakwaters, and other barriers.

PROCEDURE

Pour sand along one side of the pan so that about one-third to one-fourth of the bottom of the pan is covered to a depth of about 1 inch (2–3 cm). Slowly add water to the other side of the pan to a depth of ¾ inch (2 cm). Allow time for the water to soak into the sand. If all

Figure 36 A beach before the effects of coastal erosion; the same beach showing erosion

of the water is soaked up by the sand, add more water. Smooth the sand line out, so that it forms a relatively straight coastline.

MAKING WAVES

Before starting to experiment, you will need some practice making waves. Use a flat object such as block of wood to generate waves in the water at intervals of 1 to 2 seconds. The waves should strike the beach at about a 45-degree angle and should be strong enough to reach about halfway up the beach. Figure 37 shows the setup with a jetty (which should be left out at this point).

WAVES AND BEACHES

Once you are able to produce consistent, regular waves, smooth out the beach and start over. Continue producing the waves, and observe them and the motion and movement of the sand. What effect do the wave height and length have on the movement of sand on the beach? What changes do you observe in the coastline?

Change the angle at which the waves hit the beach as well as the wave length and height. Note any differences.

Use your model to simulate the following shoreline features: barrier islands, sandpits, tombolos, cusps, terraces, dunes, and sandbars. Examples of these shoreline features can be found in a book on geology or oceanography.

• Compare with similar features on real beaches or coastlines.

• Investigate the formation, development, and erosion of real beaches, reefs, etc., using maps, computers, experiments, interviews, etc., and study the effects on plants, animals, and humans. Look into methods used to preserve

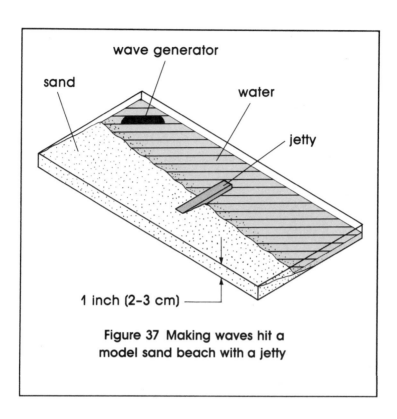

Figure 37 Making waves hit a model sand beach with a jetty

beaches, for example, designating them national sea-shores, state beaches, etc.

ARTIFICIAL SHORELINE MODIFICATION

What happens when shorelines are modified by human beings?

Use small pieces of wood, metal, gravel, rock, or glass to construct jetties (Figure 37), groins, breakwaters, sea-walls, and other structures designed to interfere with the natural action of the sea. You might even want to pour your own concrete blocks or walls.

Again produce regular waves and observe the movement of the sand. Do artificial structures affect the transport of sand?

• Compare your model structures with real artificial structures. Are these affected during storms?

BUILDING YOUR OWN WAVE GENERATOR
To free your hands and enable you to study long-term shoreline erosion, design your own wave generator, a device that generates waves automatically.

Ocean-Level Changes

Many scientists predict that the greenhouse effect will cause a rise in sea levels. Find out how this is supposed to happen and then, using topographic maps of coastlines, predict the effects of various rises in the level. What would you do to prevent the destruction of beaches, parks, cities, and homes?

• Research ocean levels and climatic changes in the past and plot current statistics on a comprehensive chart and map on which you show the complete record of such changes. Investigate any patterns you notice.

• If you are handy with a computer, you might try to write a simulation that graphically shows the changes in climate and ocean levels throughout history.

• Many parts of the United States were under the ocean at one time. If you live in, or plan to visit, one of these places, do some research on its geologic and meteorologic history. Are any features visible today that serve as clues to the ocean's presence? Account for the presence of the ocean in the past.

• Are sandy deserts and sandy beaches similar in origin? After all, both consist of sand. Look for clues to marine presence in deserts you live in or near or plan to visit.

GROUNDWATER PROJECTS

Water beneath the surface of the earth is called ground-water, and such water fills the pores and fractures in soil and rock. Groundwater can be tapped by drilling wells, and often it seeps to the surface in the form of springs. Groundwater sources supply about 35 percent of the public's water needs in the United States. Groundwater contaminated by toxic substances or other pollutants is virtually impossible to clean up.

To learn more about this vital resource and what you can do to protect it for future generations, you may want to build a model of a groundwater system.

MATERIALS

Hammer, nails, two pieces of wood 1 inch × 1 inch × 11 inches, one piece of wood 1 inch × 1 inch × 24 inches, scissors, two sheets of clear plastic ⅛ inch × 12 inches × 24 inches (3 mm × 30 cm × 76 cm), silicone rubber cement, water, ¼-inch drill, 7 feet (2 m) of rigid plastic tubing with an outer diameter of ¼ inch (6–7 mm), caulk, fine wire mesh, three pinch clamps, earth material (for example, coarse sand, silica sand, or coarse gravel), bottle, rubber hose, syringes, food coloring, modeling clay, a ¼-inch-thick rubber strip 1 inch × 12 inches (6–7 mm × 2–3 cm × 30 cm), and three 90-degree ½-inch plastic elbows. Note. Metric measurements are not used for some materials because they usually are not sold that way.

PROCEDURE

Refer to Figures 38 and 39 when following the directions.

1. Nail the two 1 inch × 1 inch × 11 inch pieces of wood to the ends of the 1 inch × 1 inch × 24 inch piece to form a three-sided frame.

2. Coat one side of the frame with the silicone rubber

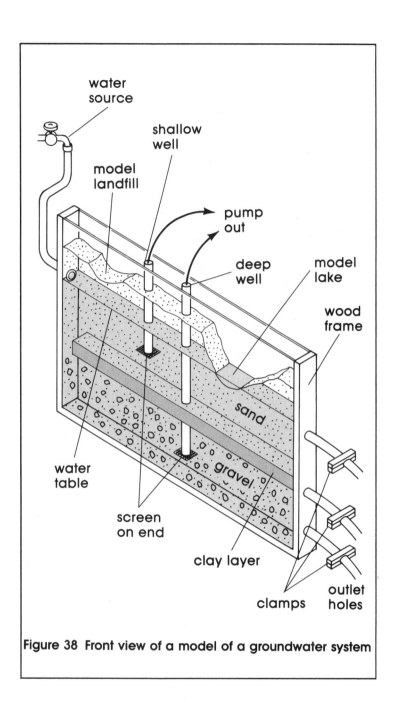

Figure 38 Front view of a model of a groundwater system

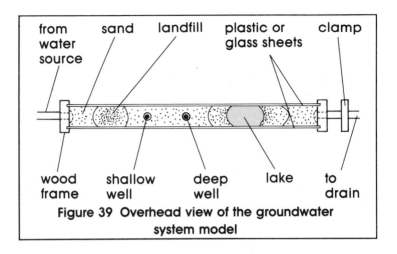

Figure 39 Overhead view of the groundwater system model

cement. Place one of the plastic sheets firmly on the frame, making sure the cement completely seals the frame with no gaps. Turn the frame over and repeat on the other side. Allow the cement to dry.

3. When the cement is dry, fill the frame with water to check for leaks. Use additional cement to fix any leaks. Empty the water when you have finished this step.

4. When your groundwater model is leakproof, drill a hole in one end of the frame about halfway up. Insert a piece of the tubing in the hole and use caulk to seal around it.

5. Drill three holes at different depths at the other end of the frame, put 2-inch (5-cm) lengths of tubing in each of these openings, and seal with caulk. Cover the opening into the holes with the fine mesh to prevent sand from going out the holes.

6. Attach a short piece of the rubber hose to each of the three tubes on the one end. Clamp off with the pinch clamps.

USING THE MODEL

Fill the model with an earth material, preferably sand in the beginning in order to learn about the basics of groundwater movement. Then add water, using the bottle attached to the hose and connected to the single tube on one side. Flow can be created by draining the water on the other end using the outlets. Wells can be simulated by using the tubing. Syringes can be used as pumps to inject impurities.

• Investigate one-directional flow from left to right. This can be modified by raising or lowering one end of the model.

• The top of the sand saturated with water is called the water table. Observe the changes in the water table as you change water flow and outlet height.

• Inject food coloring into one of the wells to allow observation of groundwater movement through the model.

• Pump water out of a well and observe the change in flow and the water table.

• Create a lake at the surface, using the rubber strip. Put some food coloring in the lake and observe its flow into the groundwater.

• Perforate the small depression (leaky lagoon) above the normal water table to simulate leakage of lagoons, landfills, or hazardous waste dumps into groundwater. Food coloring added to water makes the effects more dramatic.

• Capillary action is the movement of water in small spaces against gravity. Capillary movement can be seen causing dyes to move upward near the leaky lagoon.

As you experiment with the groundwater model you can modify it to create conditions similar to real ground-water situations. Can you create an artesian well? Can you measure the speed of the water flow? Can contaminated groundwater be cleaned?

9

EARTH—THE ULTIMATE SCIENCE PROJECT

If you have done some of the science projects suggested in this book, you should end up with a greater understanding of the structure and composition of, and processes on, the Earth. You also may understand more the idea that we are all earth scientists.

In a way, too, it can be said that the Earth itself is a science project, for it is constantly "conducting and running" experiments for us to observe and try to explain. For example, each time it rains, the Earth is running a massive condensation experiment for us to observe and learn from. Each time a river flows and moves a bit of sediment, the Earth is giving us an opportunity to learn about erosion and the transport of earth materials. Each time the wind blows or the sun shines, the Earth is performing a huge gas-mixing experiment. The Earth is the ultimate earth science laboratory, available to all those who want to use it.

An important point to consider when thinking of the Earth in this way is that we are part of the project and cannot remove ourselves from the experiment itself. Humans have introduced many new variables into the great

Earth experiment, sometimes with harmful results. Nations have depleted resources at a rate much faster than the Earth can possibly produce them, or too rapidly depleted irreplaceable resources. Humans have converted vast reserves of fossil fuels to carbon dioxide and released it into the atmosphere, upsetting the balance. We have changed the course of rivers and the shape and composition of shorelines. We have built cities next to volcanoes and on top of fault zones. We have released into the soil, water, and air massive quantities of innumerable chemicals. Each of these has the potential to alter the way the Earth works and ultimately the way we live on the Earth.

As we observe and manipulate the ultimate science project, we must listen to what the Earth is telling us and learn from it.

APPENDIX:
SCIENTIFIC SUPPLY COMPANIES, ORGANIZATIONS, AND PERIODICALS

SCIENTIFIC SUPPLY COMPANIES

Ward's Natural Science Establishment
5100 West Henrietta Road
P.O. Box 92912
Rochester, NY 14692–9012

Flinn Scientific
P.O. Box 219
131 Flinn Street
Batavia, IL 60510

ORGANIZATIONS

American Association of Petroleum Geologists
P.O. Box 979
Tulsa, OK 74101

American Geological Institute
4220 King Street
Alexandria, VA 22302–1507

American Institute of Professional Geologists
7828 Vance Drive
Arvada, CO 80003

Association for Women Geoscientists
P.O. Box 1005
Menlo Park, CA 94026

Association of Engineering Geologists
62 King Philip Road
Sudbury, MA 01776

Geological Society of America
3300 Penrose Place
P.O. Box 9140
Boulder, CO 80301

Mineralogical Society of America
1625 I Street NW
Suite 414
Washington, DC

National Association of Geology Teachers
P.O. Box 368
Lawrence, KS 66044

National Earth Science Teachers Association
Department of Geological Sciences
Michigan State University
East Lansing, MI 48824

National Speleological Society
1 Cave Avenue
Huntsville, AL 35810

Paleontological Society
U.S. Geological Survey
E-501
U.S. National Museum
Washington, DC 20560

Seismological Society of America
6431 Geological Avenue
El Cerrito, CA 94530

Society of Economists, Paleontologists &
Mineralogists
P.O. Box 4756
Tulsa, OK 74159–0756

Society of Mining Engineers
8307 Parkway
P.O. Box 625002
Littleton, CO 80162–9550

Society of Vertebrate Paleontology
Los Angeles County Museum of Natural History
900 Exposition Boulevard
Los Angeles, CA 90007

U.S. Geological Survey
P.O. Box 25286
Federal Center
Denver, CO 80225

PERIODICALS

Earth Science
American Geological Institute
4220 King St.
Alexandria, VA 22302–1507

Lapidary Journal
1094 Cudahy Place
San Diego, CA 92110

Rocks and Minerals
Heldref Publications
4000 Albemarle St. NW
Washington, DC 20016

FOR FURTHER READING

Chapter 1

General Background in Geology

American Geological Institute. *Dictionary of Geological Terms.* Garden City, N.Y.: Doubleday (Anchor Press), 1976.

Lambert, David, and The Diagram Group. *The Field Guide to Geology.* New York: Facts on File, 1989.

Rhodes, Frank H. T. *Geology.* A Golden Nature Guide. New York: Golden Press, 1971.

Science Projects and Science Fairs

Beller, Joel. *So You Want to Do a Science Fair Project.* New York: Arco, 1982.

Heller, Robert E. *Geology and Earth Science Sourcebook for Elementary and Secondary Schools.* New York: Holt, Rinehart and Winston, 1970.

Tocci, Salvatore. *How to Do a Science Fair Project.* New York: Watts, 1986.

Van Deman, Barry A., and McDonald, Ed. *Nuts and Bolts: A Matter of Fact Guide to Science Fair Projects.* Harwood Heights, Ill.: The Science Man Press, 1982.

Chapter 2

Gay, Kathlyn. *Science in Ancient Greece.* New York: Franklin Watts, 1988.

Harris, Jacqueline L. *Science in Ancient Rome.* New York: Franklin Watts, 1988.

Chapter 3

Brown, Vinson. *Building Your Own Nature Museum for Study and Pleasure.* New York: Arco, 1984.

Chesterman, Charles W. *The Audubon Society Guide to Rocks and Minerals.* New York: Knopf, 1979.

MacFarlane, Ruth B. *Making Your Own Nature Museum.* New York: Franklin Watts, 1989.

Pough, Fredrick H. *A Field Guide to Rocks and Minerals.* Fourth ed. Boston: Houghton Mifflin, 1983.

Rhodes, Frank H. T., Zim, Herbert S., and Shaffer, Paul R. *Fossils.* A Golden Nature Guide. New York: Golden Press, 1962.

Sorrell, Charles. *Rocks and Minerals.* A Golden Field Guide. New York: Golden Press, 1974.

Thompson, Ida. *The Audubon Society Field Guide to North American Fossils.* New York: Knopf, 1982.

Chapter 4

Holden, Alan, and Singer, Phyllis. *Crystals and Crystal Growing.* Cambridge, Mass.: The MIT Press, 1982.

Hurlbut, C. S., Jr., and Klein, Cornelius. *Manual of Mineralogy.* Nineteenth ed. New York: John Wiley & Sons, 1977.

Chapter 5

Eicher, D. L. *Geologic Time.* Englewood Cliffs, N.J.: Prentice-Hall, 1968.

McAlester, A. L. *The History of Life.* Englewood Cliffs, N.J.: Prentice-Hall, 1968.

Mintz, L. W. *Historical Geology.* 2nd Ed. Columbus, Ohio: Charles E. Merrill, 1977.

Chapter 6

Aylesworth, Thomas. *The Mount St. Helens Disaster: What We've Learned.* New York: Franklin Watts, 1983.

Bullard, F. M. *Volcanoes of the Earth.* Austin, Tx.: University of Texas Press, 1976.

Dalrymple, G. B. et al. "Origin of the Hawaiian Islands." *American Scientist.* May–June 1973. Vol. 61, No. 3, pp. 294–308.

Hodgson, James H. *Earthquakes and Earth Structure.* Englewood Cliffs, N.J.: Prentice-Hall, 1964.

Lauber, Patricia. *Volcano. The Eruption and Healing of Mount St. Helens.* New York: Bradbury Press, 1986.

Chapter 7

Dewey, J. F. "Plate Tectonics." *Scientific American.* May 1972. Vol. 226, No. 5, pp. 56–68.

Hallam, A. "Continental Drift and the Fossil Record." *Scientific American.* November 1972. Vol. 227, No. 5, pp. 56–66.

Rossbacher, Lisa A. *Recent Revolutions in Geology.* New York: Franklin Watts, 1986.

Wilson, Tuzo J. "Continental Drift." *Scientific American.* April 1963.

Chapter 8

Bascom, Willard. *Waves and Beaches: The Dynamics of the Ocean Surface.* Garden City, N.Y.: Doubleday, 1964.

Bloom, A. L. *The Surface of the Earth.* Englewood Cliffs, N.J.: Prentice-Hall, 1969.

Olson, Ralph E. *The Geography of Water.* Dubuque, Iowa: William C. Brown, 1970.

INDEX